System Program Exercises in Data Processing

W. SKOK, MSc., MBCS

Senior Lecturer in Computing
Polytechnic of the South Bank.

D.P. PUBLICATIONS
16 Bere Close
Winchester, Hampshire SO22 5HY
1982

ACKNOWLEDGEMENTS

The author gratefully acknowledges the co-operation and assistance of the following organisations and persons in preparing this text:

The Department of the Environment for permission to base the Driving Test Booking System Case Study around the operations that they undertake.

Mr N. B. Dyson for his ideas concerning the Telephone Invoicing System Case Study.

Members of the Computer Studies Division, of Ealing College of Higher Education, for their helpful comments.

Mr P. Smith of Oxford Polytechnic, for reading through the manuscript and making many helpful comments and suggestions.

Also to the many students who through their dedicated efforts have contributed to the development and improvement of the exercises presented within.

ISBN 0 905435 30 3

Copyright W. SKOK © 1982

Printed in Great Britain by
Spottiswoode Ballantyne Ltd
Colchester, Essex

Preface

AIM

1. To give a *full* understanding of Data Processing by providing the means to build on textbook knowledge in a practical way.

2. It is intended for the following students:

a. Those taking Data Processing or Systems Analysis as part of a CNAA or university degree course.

b. Those taking Computing Studies as part of a BEC/TEC Diploma or Certificate.

c. Chartered, Certified and Cost and Management Accountancy examinees in Data Processing – the Systems Exercises are particularly useful to them.

d. Students taking City and Guilds 746 and 747 Computer Programming and Information Processing Certificates.

e. Those taking any course in which there is a requirement for a programming project, eg GCE 'O' level.

NEED

3. The need was seen for a set of exercises, which would give the student an insight into *practical* problems involved in designing, implementing and running computer-based data processing systems.

APPROACH

4. Assumed knowledge is that gained via the teaching/study of Data Processing to the level of a basic textbook on the subject such as 'Data Processing' by Oliver and Chapman (of this publisher).

Exercises in Systems and Programming give the student a *full understanding* of a topic. This is achieved by allowing the student to consider the topic *in a practical business situation to which he can readily identify*.

USE

5. Primarily it is intended to be used in the classroom situation *in conjunction* with a textbook on Data Processing. However, it can be of tremendous benefit to students studying alone.

CONTENT

6. The exercises are of two types – those *with answers* which can be used in the classroom situation to show the student *what* is required of him and for the student studying alone to check his own answer. Also exercises *without* answers provided in the book; (in this case, the answers are available to lecturers applying to the publishers on departmental headed notepaper). This second type of exercise may be used either in the classroom situation or on an assignment basis, in order to give a challenge to the student and to create classroom discussion.

The text is split into four parts:

Part I   Systems Exercises
Part II   Programming Exercises
Part III   Suggested Solutions to Selected Systems Exercises
Part IV   Suggested Solutions to Selected Programming Exercises

PART I – SYSTEMS EXERCISES

7. This presents exercises from basic questions on data processing principles to overall file design and processing considerations in a comprehensive system. The first eight questions which are marked with an asterisk have suggested answers in Part III. The answers are not taken directly from actual situations and are not intended to be a definitive statement of a unique solution, but are intended to provide an example of a workable solution.

Some questions in the longer assignments have a mark allocation, in order to assist the evaluation of student's work.

The *sequence* of the exercises is designed to be compatible with that which might be encountered in a typical data processing course. However, the lecturer may set individual exercises as and when required, since they are *totally independent*.

The number of exercises provided is more than a student would be expected to undertake in a single year of study, but the wide choice will facilitate revision and self-study.

PART II – PROGRAMMING EXERCISES

8. In this section, eleven practical exercises are set, so that the student may see realistic data processing problems in a simplified environment, which he can understand.

An initial introduction to the BASIC programming language is assumed, so that exercises may be set as coursework assignments or to provide programming examples. Alternatively the questions may be dealt with as flowcharting exercises. (The program flowchart symbols are shown in Appendix B). BASIC was chosen as it is widely available on mainframe, mini and micro-computer configurations and is both easy to learn and use.

In all cases the programs are intended to demonstrate a fairly realistic company or administrative requirement, but simplification, eg non-complicated record structures, has been made for clarity and ease of understanding. However, at all times the student is made aware, and gains an understanding of, the *important concepts*.

Questions with an asterisk have suggested answers in Part IV. These answers may take the form of a program explanation, program flowchart, source code, output or data file listing. The program listings are intended to demonstrate working solutions, that a student would be expected to produce. The PRIME version of BASIC has been used in the source code listings and the major differences from other versions are given at the end of Appendix D.

The BASIC language is used in the text to illustrate a possible solution, but this does not imply that the use of BASIC is the only, or even the best, way of implementing the solutions.

W. SKOK
May 1982

Table of Contents

Part I

Systems Exercises

Introduction

Many data processing students are employed on a full-time or sandwich basis and their view of data processing systems is geared specifically to an employer's use of such systems. In most cases the student acts as a user of computer systems; either as a direct user ie data input, program writing or using software packages, or as an indirect user ie receiving computer generated reports on which to take action or make decisions.

In order to appreciate the way in which such systems function, the student must be aware and have experience of a number of important concepts. The main concepts are:–

1. File and record structures

2. The logical sequence involved in processing transaction data against previously recorded data.

3. Principles of data processing eg data validation techniques, back-up procedures etc.

In his day to day work, the student need not concern himself with physical data organisation on the computer hardware devices. Such knowledge forms part of the requirements of the various examination bodies, but is not dealt with in this text. In fact, the exercises in the text are designed to be highly practical, to cover the above three concepts and also the logical problems, which may be encountered in setting up and running systems on:–

a. main-frame or mini installations

b. A micro-computer based installation, whether it is located in the firm, educational establishment or at home.

As such, they are also useful to an employee who wishes to learn more about how a computer system operates in practice, as well as to students sitting examinations in data processing.

It is expected that the student would already have received supporting lectures and wishes to test his knowledge in a practical way.

The exercises are classified by the time an average student would normally take. Exercises 1-9 are designed to last up to one hour; these could cover a weekly tutorial period. The time required for the essay questions in Exercise 10 will depend very much on the preliminary work done by the lecturer, since the areas covered are of a very practical nature. Exercises 11-15 are designed to cover a longer duration and might be used as assignments, for which the student would need to undertake some detailed investigation and study.

One of the most important parts of system documentation is the system flowchart, which assists in clearly showing the overall flow of data between

1

the source documents, files and reports. It is one of the most powerful means of understanding the operation of a data processing system and so the exercises include considerable practice in their construction.

The exercises involving system flowcharts are of three types:–

a. Evaluation and understanding of given system flowcharts and symbols.

b. Flowcharting of an existing system.

c. Flowcharting of a new system, where the user may decide on file and reporting requirements.

The system flowchart symbols are defined in Appendix A and, as an example, a complete system flowchart for a simplified payroll run is given in Appendix C.

1 Company Application Areas*

Note: The asterisk denotes that an answer to the exercise is to be found in Part III.

For each of the following types of companies, list the main business areas within that company, that might benefit from the use of computer based systems.

    a. National airline
    b. Food manufacturer
    c. Local authority
    d. National Magazine publisher
    e. Local Estate Agent

For each area, list some of the computer reports that could be generated.

NOTES: *1. The business areas might include company operations, such as sales, production, purchasing, finance etc.*
    2. This exercise will require quite detailed investigation on the part of the student and therefore not all the above types of companies need be examined by each student.

3

2 Types of DP Files*

Describe the Files that would be necessary for each of the following computer systems. Your answer should include: name of file, a selection of typical contents of a record, the record key and type of file, eg

Customer File;

Customer Account Number – *Record Key*, Name and Address, Credit Limit;

Master File.

The method of working or any special requirements should also be stated, eg real time updating.

a. A payroll system for a large company.

b. A mail-order system which receives orders from agents, checks which items are in stock, produces a file of ordered items in stock and then prints invoices (by referring to a file of agents names and address).

c. A police system for recording details of stolen cars and answering queries from on-duty police officers.

d. A computer dating agency, which matches applicants' requirements with previously stored data relating to other people.

e. A large shipping company which has a system to locate ships and keeps details of cargo, destination, insurance etc.

NOTE: *There are four types of files used in computer-based data processing systems. They are:*

1. **Master File** – *containing main records of the system.*

2. **Transaction File** – *containing details of movements (or transactions) that have taken place since the master file was last updated.*

3. **Common Data (or Reference File)** – *containing data that is common to all records in the system.*

4. **Working File** – *temporary files created within a process and not retained after the process.*

3 Job Functions of a Systems Analyst*

The work undertaken by a systems analyst varies from company to company and depends on company size and application area. The aim of this exercise is to list the possible *functions* that a systems analyst could undertake, by scanning the job adverts for systems analysts in the computer press.

For example, the advert below contains the following tasks:

"to evaluate existing work functions";

"meeting departmental staff at all levels";

"outlining and designing computer systems".

Systems Analysts

If you're seriously trying to build a career as a Systems Analyst then you'll know that getting to the top largely depends on the range of experience you can acquire. There's an opportunity to broaden your working knowledge by coming to work for us.

Running major manufacturing plants is a complex business. We believe that computers can play a vital role in maintaining the scope and quality of information being used by Management to control the running of all the plants that we own in the U.K.

We're looking for Systems Analysts, based in Middlesex, to help us evaluate existing work functions and to design computer systems which can provide people with up-to-date information at the push of a button. A Senior Systems Analyst will determine which project areas you will investigate for possible computer development. Your work will involve meeting departmental staff at all levels to discover the specific problem areas to be analysed and resolved. Later you will be responsible for outlining and designing computer systems.

You should have 1-2 years experience in Systems Analysis and must have programming experience using Cobol.

All the responsibility
you can handle!

Also, make a summary of the previous work experience required by the adverts.

For example, from above advert the requirement is for 1-2 year systems analysis experience and programming experience in COBOL.

What conclusions can you draw about the type of previous experience needed?

4 Computerisation Studies*

a. HOTEL COMPUTERISATION STUDY

A five star hotel in Park Lane has 500 rooms, three restaurants, four bars, a hairdressing salon, a laundry, ten shops, room service and a recreational complex. The available staff numbers 100.

The present manual system for preparing bills allows hotel clients to sign a card whenever they make use of a hotel service. The card shows room number, service details, location, date, time and cost of service. The cards are collected at various times of the day and sent to the accounts desk, where the bill is made up. The client makes one covering payment at the time of departure.

For some time, the hotel manager has received numerous queries and complaints from clients regarding their bills. So he asked an independent computer consultancy to study the feasibility of introducing a computer system to replace the manual one.

The consultants' report is complete and includes a recommendation for a mini-computer system with terminals at each possible service point.

a. List the benefits to the hotel that might have been included in the consultants' report.

b. Describe the stages that would be necessary to make the computer system operational (Assume no appropriate software packages exist).

c. Describe the likely problems that might occur once the system is running and state what measures could be taken to prevent them or minimise their effect.

d. List other areas that the system could be extended to cover.

b. SUPERMARKET COMPUTERISATION STUDY

A supermarket is considering replacing its cash registers by a point-of-sale (POS) computer based system. Each store in the chain would purchase a mini-computer with terminals to each check-out counter, where laser reading devices would price customers' purchases. The Stock File would be held on magnetic disc backing store and a line printer would be used to prepare management reports.

Management insist that all necessary activities for implementation of the system, such as hardware selection, hardware purchase, system development and testing, should be completed within a two year period. They also recommend the use of software packages wherever possible.

i. Describe the potential benefits to the supermarket of installing such a system.

ii. Draw up a detailed plan, in the form of a barchart, for implementation of the system, within the time-scale demanded by management.

iii. Describe the likely effects on the supermarket staff of the introduction of such a system.

iv. Describe the problems that may arise once the system is operational.

5 Introductory System Flowchart Exercises*

a. MATCHING SITUATIONS WITH SYMBOLS

System Flowchart extracts covering ten situations commonly encountered in data processing systems are shown on the next page. The descriptions of all the situations are given below.

Match each description with the system flowchart to which it best corresponds.

Insert
Flowchart
number

A Building Society counter clerk requests customers details via a teletype terminal. ☐

A supermarket manager's orders (held on an OMR document) are input into a computer system. ☐

An Employee File (held on magnetic tape) is sorted into Employee Number order. ☐

Stock transactions (held on magnetic tape) are used to update a Stock Master File (also held on magnetic tape). ☐

A credit card company's transactions are converted to microfilm prior to being processed via a key-to-tape machine. ☐

Data from a payroll calculation is output onto a disc for later printing of payslips. ☐

Clock cards are converted to punched cards. ☐

Payments (held on magnetic tape) are used to update a Sales Ledger (held on magnetic disc). ☐

Orders are input and validated using a key-to-disc system, which writes the valid data to magnetic tape and prints an invalid order report. ☐

A message is output via the operator's console to indicate the completion of the weekly sales analysis. ☐

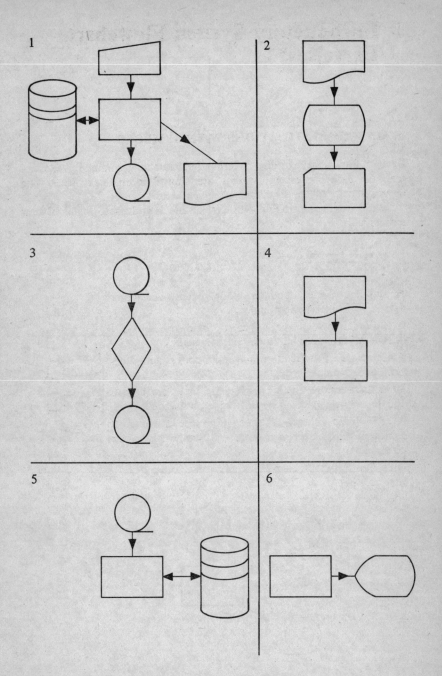

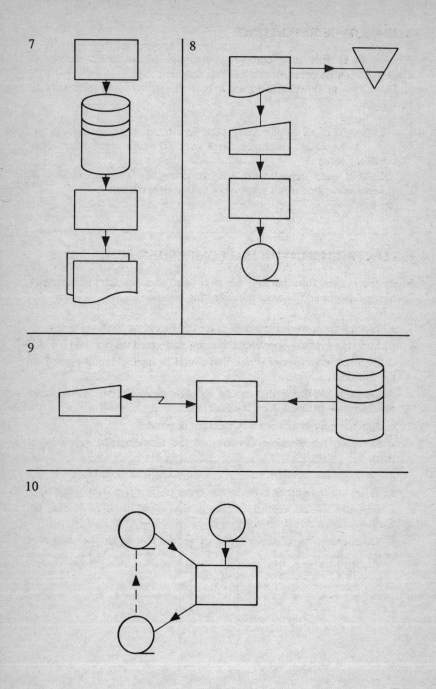

b. EMPLOYEE REPORTING

An Employee File in a company personnel system holds records in employee number order, and is held on magnetic tape.

Draw system flowcharts to show how the following reports may be produced.

    i. A list of all employees in each department in alphabetical order.

    ii. A list of all employees with over 20 years service in alphabetical order.

    iii. For each department, a figure giving the average number of years of service of all employees in that department.

c. ELECTRICITY INVOICING COMPREHENSION

Study the system flowchart on the next page of a simplified Electricity Invoicing System and answer the following questions.

    a. In what form would the data enter the Invoicing System?

    b. State the manual operations that are performed on the data.

    c. Describe the types of errors that would be highlighted at point 1 on the flowchart.

    d. Describe the steps that would be necessary in order to undertake the operation at point 2 on the flowchart.

    e. Explain why a sort run is necessary at point 3.

    f. Describe the possible contents of the Customer Master File at point 4.

    g. Describe the possible contents of the disc file at point 5.

    h. What are the names given to the types of files at points 5 and 6?

    i. Describe the file security measures that could be taken in case the Customer Master File is corrupted.

    j. Give examples of three types of report that might be output at point 7.

System Flowchart for Simplified Electricity Invoicing System

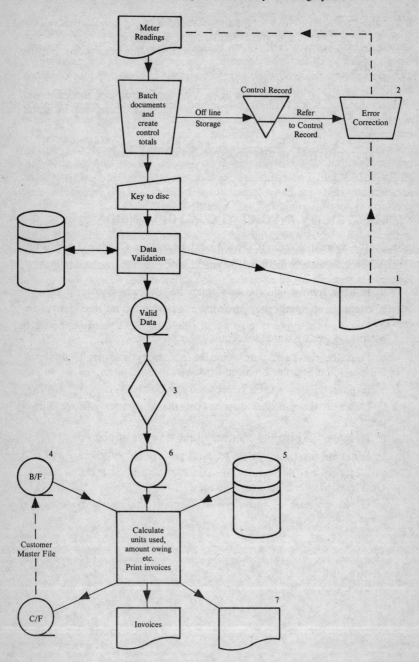

d. PRODUCTION CONTROL

Draw a *system* flowchart for the following system:

An engineering company has a computerised production control system, which keeps a JOB file on magnetic tape. The JOB file contains details of all work for each contract to be carried out in the production department eg a piece of work might be cutting to shape and drilling 100 metal blocks. The file is in job number within contract number order.

Each piece of work (or job) has a "work progress sheet" giving details of all operations to be carried out and on which the production operator enters details of the work he has done.

When a job leaves the production department, a punched card is produced from the "work progress sheet" and this forms the PROGRESS file. The cards are input to the system, where valid cards are written onto magnetic tape. Invalid cards are corrected by the production controller and re-input into the system.

The magnetic tape file is then used to update the JOB file. During the update a list of jobs which have been fully completed is made. Any jobs of that run, that have only been partly completed are written onto a JOB QUERY file, which is held on magnetic disc. A "Management Query Report" is then produced from the JOB QUERY file.

The JOB file is periodically checked in order to produce a "Contract Status" report, showing the percentage of jobs completed for each contract.

Controls are incorporated throughout the process.

6 Office Cleaning Firm*

An office cleaning firm has approximately 500 clients and uses a mini-computer system to handle the timing of work carried out by its staff.

Initially clients sign a contract (which is retained in the general manager's office for reference) and this information is introduced into the computer system via a visual display unit. Any input errors are displayed on the screen, corrected and re-input as soon as possible.

Every four weeks a print-out is produced showing the work to be carried out during the next four weeks. This print-out includes floor-area to be cleaned, type of cleaning and any special requirements. At the same time an invoice file is created, from which invoices are later printed out and sent to the clients.

In addition a summary of work for the following four week period (ie 5 to 8 weeks ahead) is printed to enable the manager to schedule his staff and foresee any potential difficulties. Staff details are kept on a manual system.

Payments made to the firm are always input immediately and used to update the master file. (A manual record is also kept in the general manager's office).

The computer system uses just one master file and the configuration consists of:

- central processor unit
- two magnetic disc drives
- two visual display units
- lineprinter

a. Describe the possible contents of the master file, which would be necessary for the computer-based system.

b. Draw a *system* flowchart for the computer-based system, showing clearly which parts are carried out:
  i.   at irregular intervals, and
  ii. every four weeks

c. Describe how the staffing details in the manual system might be introduced into the computer system and for what purposes they might be used.

7 Property Company System*

A property company owns a large number of offices throughout the country. Clients lease these offices and make a quarterly payment to the company. The company has decided to computerise the system for collection of payments.

Design a computer-based system, which would be appropriate for this application; and undertake the following tasks for the system you have designed:

a. List the fields that you would expect would be held in the master file of the computer-based system. (Assume that a client does not lease more than one office).

b. Suggest a storage device that would be appropriate for the master file, and state the reasons for your suggestion.

c. Draw a *system* flowchart to cover procedures to input payments, update the file, produce payment receipts and provide summary reports.

8 Baby-Sitter System*

A self employed accountant lives on a new housing estate, on which most families have young children. The Residents' Association asked him to start up and organise a baby-sitting circle to cover 150 families. The main aim was to keep a record of people who would baby-sit in exchange for someone else looking after their children when they went out. The system would also regularly update this record.

The accountant had a micro-computer, which he used for his consultancy, and he was proficient in BASIC. His configuration was as follows: visual display unit, micro-processor unit, printer and a twin floppy disc drive.

He decided to develop a micro-computer based system to keep a record of baby-sitting requirements, bookings, availability and "time-credit" figures. The system would use a Family Master File, which would be held on floppy disc.

a. Describe the possible contents of the Family Master File.

b. Suggest a scheme for allocating "time-credits" for work carried out.

c. Draw a system flowchart to cover procedures for requesting a baby-sitter, printing out of schedules and updating the master file.

9 Private Health Insurance System

A private health service company operates a number of independent hospitals and a private health scheme. Members make monthly or annual subscriptions into the scheme and whenever they or their dependant relatives require hospital treatment, they contact any of the company's branch offices and make arrangements to see a hospital consultant.

The company have a central computer system, which holds the main Member records and is linked to each branch office.

The Members Master File contains the following:

1. Registration Number (Ten digits)
2. Date of Registration
3. Title
4. First Names
5. Surname
6. Address
7. Postcode
8. Telephone Number
9. Date of Birth
10. Occupation
11. Scale of Cover (eg London or National)
12. Amount of Monthly Payment
13. Date of Last Payment
14. Date Last Payment Due
15. Total Payment in Current Registration Year
16. Dependant Relatives (one record per relative)

    a. First Names
    b. Surname
    c. Date of Birth
    d. Relationship to Insured Member

Whenever staff at the branch office make an enquiry the system validates and processes the request for information.

a. Describe how the Members Registration Number might be validated.

b. Design report layouts (suitable for display on a Visual Display Unit) which could be used for replies to branch enquiries concerning:
    i. Member's current status regarding payment into the scheme.
    ii. Details of Member's dependant relatives.

17

10 Essays

a. DP DEPARTMENT V USER DEPARTMENT

The managing director of a large manufacturing company was quoted as saying:

"Our computer projects are always months behind schedule. The DP Manager blames the user departments, while the users criticise the DP department".

a. Discuss the reasons that users and the DP department might have difficulties in reaching a good working relationship in the above company.

b. Describe the problems that may arise in the company because of this poor relationship.

c. Recommend the measures that might be taken in order to improve the user/DP department relationship.

b. MICROPROCESSING DEVELOPMENTS

Describe the main application areas that have and will be affected by recent developments in microprocessing.

Analyse and discuss the likely effects of these developments in each area that you have described.

c. CENTRALISATION V DE-CENTRALISATION

At a recent board meeting the chief accountant of an international manufacturing company was quoted as saying, "We have had so many problems with our centralised DP Department that I should like to propose the widespread use of micro-computers within all departments, as a better alternative".

Describe the typical problems that may be encountered with a centralised DP department, and list the likely advantages and disadvantages of introducing micro-computers to all departments.

d. SYSTEM DESIGN FAILURES

The following press statement concerning the computerising of the vehicle licence centre at Swansea was recently made:

"The real failures there were not technical, but rather inadequate management at the outset at a senior level and insufficiently comprehensive systems design"

Give examples of where this system might have had failures and explain how the problems quoted above might have contributed to such failures.

18

11 Off-Licence Chain System

A company which operates a chain of off-licences in the South East of England uses a computer-based system to aid in the running of its operations.

A fleet of delivery vans distribute products (eg spirits, wine, soft drinks, mixers, snacks etc.) from a central warehouse in East London to all the company's off-licences. On a specific day in the month each shop manager receives a delivery, gives the van driver a completed order form for the next delivery and retains a copy of the order in his office. The order form consists of an Optical Mark Reading (OMR) document, which the manager completes by inserting pencil marks to indicate the quantities of each item required.

The van driver collects all order forms and these are returned to the computer centre, which is located at the central warehouse. (The main-frame computer configuration includes magnetic tape and disc backing storage).

The order forms are entered into the computer system, where a check is made against the Stock Master File (held on magnetic disc) in order to produce a "picking" list (showing item code, description, quantity, van driver number, delivery date and warehouse location).

Items not in stock are written onto a Stock-Out File (held on magnetic tape) and from this a report is printed in supplier code sequence, showing the insufficient quantities.

   a.   State the advantages of using OMR documents for input in the above application.

   b.   Describe the possible contents of the Stock Master File.

   c.   Draw a *system* flowchart for (i) Order Processing, and (ii) Stock File Maintenance.

   d.   Suggest a procedure for dealing with orders, which are only partly filled.

12 Library System

INTRODUCTION
A newly appointed DP Manager has been asked to install, design and implement a complete computer-based system for the central public library of a local authority. The DP Manager must decide the hardware requirements, the files to be kept and the processing that has to be carried out.

DESCRIPTION OF LIBRARY OPERATION
The central library is supported by 12 branch libraries and is responsible for:–
  i.   Maintenance of a Master Catalogue.
  ii. Orders and payments for new books.
  iii. Maintenance of records of loans to the public, branch libraries and libraries outside the local authority.
  iv. Processing and requests via National Lending Library.

The present manual system is inefficient and it is hoped that a new computer system will improve the operating procedures. The procedures are divided into scheduled and on-demand operations and are now described.

Scheduled Operations
  a. To process (daily) the loan and return of books.
  b. To print (annually) the Master Catalogue of all the books.
  c. To print (monthly) a list of purchases and withdrawals from the stock of books.
  d. To print (weekly) a list of books loaned to libraries outside the local authority.
  e. To print orders for new books from publishers and to issue payments when books are received (weekly).

On-demand Operations
  f. To print a list of overdue books with reminders to readers.
  g. To process requests for books from the branch libraries.
  h. To print a list of books, classified by Author, Title, Subject or ISBN.

ASSIGNMENT
1. Draw a block diagram outlining the hardware configuration that would be required for this system.

2. State the files that would be required and describe their possible contents.

3. Draw system flowcharts to cover the scheduled *and* on-demand operations (a), (f) and (g).

13 Driving Test Booking System

a. DESCRIPTION

Applications for driving test appointments in the Metropolitan Traffic area are made on form DL26(M), which is obtainable from any Post Office in the London area, and sent to the Traffic Area Office at Acton. This office receives the forms, checks that the money and entries on the form are correct and then gathers the forms together in a batch of about one hundred. Each batch is divided into ordinary applications and priority applications ie those who wish to obtain a cancellation at short notice. A further type of input is notifications of cancellations and results. At the end of a day each batch is stamped with a batch number and these are sent down to the computer centre at Brighton.

The computer-based system deals with the allocation of driving test dates and master file maintenance and is now described.

The source documents are converted to disc, via a key-to-disc system, which is worked by twenty operators at individual key stations.

As the main backing storage device in the computer installation is magnetic tape, the next stage is the conversion of the data from disc to tape. The data gathered in this way between Mondays and Thursdays is used for the weekly updating of the History Master File on Fridays. About ten thousand transactions are processed weekly in this way.

The History Master File, which is held on magnetic tape in driving licence number order, contains details of previous tests over the last five years and the results eg pass, fail, cancelled or failure to turn up.

The update run calculates appointment dates and examiner lists; this data is written onto magnetic disc for later printing of appointment cards (see below) and the examiner's day journal ie lists of dates and times for conducting tests at each test centre in the Metropolitan Area (see page 4 of Application Form).

At the end of the month a report is printed showing the pass rates (for that month) for each driving test centre in test centre code order.

Every three months a file maintenance run deletes records, which are greater than five years old.

b. ASSIGNMENT

Read the Driving Test Booking System description, obtain an application form from a Post Office and answer the following questions.

21

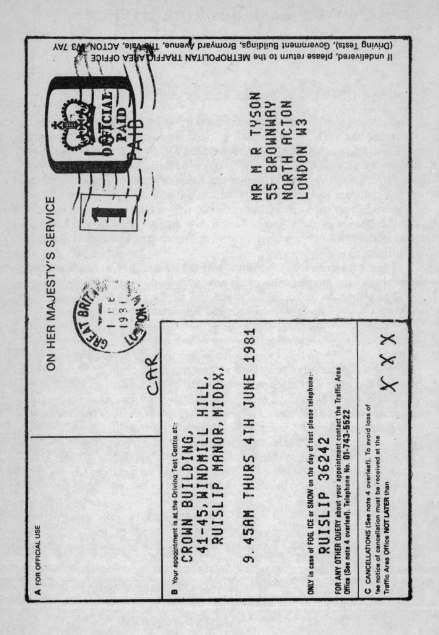

If undelivered, please return to the METROPOLITAN TRAFFIC AREA OFFICE (Driving Tests), Government Buildings, Bromyard Avenue, The Vale, ACTON, W3 7AY

ON HER MAJESTY'S SERVICE

OFFICIAL PAID

MR M R TYSON
55 BROWNWAY
NORTH ACTON
LONDON W3

GREAT BRITAIN
1981
EUSTON W.

CAR

A FOR OFFICIAL USE

B Your appointment is at the Driving Test Centre at:-

CROWN BUILDING,
41-45, WINDMILL HILL,
RUISLIP MANOR, MIDDX,

9.45AM THURS 4TH JUNE 1981

ONLY in case of FOG, ICE or SNOW on the day of test please telephone:-

RUISLIP 36242

FOR ANY OTHER QUERY about your appointment contact the Traffic Area Office (See note 4 overleaf). Telephone No. 01-743-5522

C CANCELLATIONS (See note 4 overleaf). To avoid loss of fee notice of cancellation must be received at the Traffic Area Office **NOT LATER** than

X X X

Example of Appointment Card

22

1. List the fields that you would expect to be held in the History Master File.
(10 marks)

2. Describe the controls that could be incorporated on a batch of application forms and the data validation checks that could be performed on the transaction data. (10 marks)

3. Describe the contents of any Reference File that may be needed during the update run. (5 marks)

4. Draw a *system* flowchart for each of the following procedures:

    a.   Processing of Application Forms and associated data.

    b.   Printing of Driving Centre Pass Rate Reports.

    c.   History File Maintenance run.

(Annotate freely in order to explain exactly what takes place during any particular run). (35 marks)

5. Suggest the possible contents of the examiners' day journal, by showing the format of the printed report. (This should give the exact layout of all the data items in the report). (10 marks)

6. Describe the measures that could be taken to protect the History Master File against loss or corruption. (5 marks)

7. If the line printer operates at a speed of 2000 lpm, with an average skip rate of 10 milliseconds, how long would it take to print out 10000 appointment cards, which comprise:

    three lines giving test centre address
    one line gap
    one line giving test date and applicant name
    four lines giving applicant address
    one line giving test centre telephone number
    ten line gap to next card (5 marks)

8. Short Answer Section (2 marks each)

    a.   Which field on the application form identifies the applicant uniquely?

    b.   State the name of the type of software, which would carry out the disc to tape conversion.

    c.   Give the title of the position of the person in the dp department, who would be responsible for control over use and storage of the History magnetic tape reels.

    d.   State two advantages of using a key-to-disc system for data entry.

    e.   When master files on magnetic tape are updated, the files are said to be updated by:

     i.   overwriting, or

     ii. copying

Select the correct term (i) or (ii).

f.   Name a programming language that would be suitable for this application.

g.   State the term used to describe the output of the results of a run onto backing store for later printing.

h.   Suggest a coding scheme for Question 6 on the Application Form ie Unacceptable days of the week.

i.   Suggest how the data held on the History File might be useful to the Driver and Vehicle Licensing Centre (DVLC) at Swansea.

j.   Suggest how the data held on the History File might be useful if the Government introduced a law requiring a probationary licence for one year after passing the driving test.

14 Mail Order Company

a. INTRODUCTION

A mail order company is concerned with selling an extremely wide range of goods through the postal service to its agents. As well as his own purchases, an agent is expected to obtain as many orders as possible from friends, relatives and colleagues at work. The agent receives a commission of about 10% of the selling price for all orders made.

The agent's method of making a sale is via a catalogue which may consist of about 500 pages illustrated in colour and depicting the items for sale. These items range from clothes, household equipment, sports equipment to children's toys and games. Each item has a unique reference number known as the catalogue number and this is used at all the stages in the data processing operations. These stages commence with the agent filling in details of the items he or she requires, and then include the clerical and computer processing at the mail order company's offices. The stages are completed when the goods arrive by post at the agent's home, together with an invoice outlining the amount required. The agent is then required to make payments which may be on a weekly or fortnightly basis through the bank transfer system.

b. DESCRIPTION

INTRODUCTION

A mail order company has a computer based system to aid in the running of its operations. The system has three master files:

    i. **Agent File**, which is held on magnetic disc, organised indexed sequentially in agent number order.

    ii. **Stock File**, which is held on magnetic tape, in catalogue number order.

    iii. **Supplier and Price File**, which is held on magnetic disc, organised indexed sequentially in catalogue number order.

The overall system consists of a number of sub-systems, which are now described.

    a. **Order Processing.** Orders are received from agents on the following form:

ORDER FORM

MRS P SMYTHE   AGENT NO.   102 2469 6
45 SPRINGWOOD GARDENS
HOPWOOD LANE
HALIFAX W YORKSHIRE
HX3 0TQ

Page No	Catalogue No	Qty	Colour	Article	Size	Price Each £ p		Total Price £ p	

At 2.00 pm all orders received during that day are collected together in a batch and sent to the data preparation room for transfer to magnetic tape. The orders are then validated and a check is made against the Stock File, in order to see which items are available. Items which are available are recorded on an Invoice File (held on magnetic tape), while items out of stock are listed on a "Stock Out" Report and an emergency ordering procedure is instigated.

The Invoice File is processed sequentially against the Agent File in order to prepare the final invoices, which also include any previous ordered items that have not yet been fully paid for.

b.   **Agent Payments**. Payments from agents are processed prior to the order processing runs and are used to update the Agent File. A "Payment Summary" Report is printed out, showing all valid payments in that run in agent number order.

c.   **Agent File Maintenance**. Every morning any agent changes are recorded onto an "Agent Change" form, and this data is used to update the Agent File. The changes may include:
   i.   New Agents added to the file.
   ii.   Modification of agent details eg name, address, credit limit.
   iii.   Deletion of agents, who no longer wish to take the catalogue.
With (iii) above, a check is made to ensure that departing agents have no outstanding debts; (in the case of an outstanding debt a report giving the appropriate details is printed).

d.   **Stock File Maintenance**. Every Friday morning, any changes to the Stock File, such as, items received from suppliers, addition of new lines, modification of stock record details or deletion of items, is made. During this run a "Stock Changes" Report is printed out for the Warehouse Manager, giving a list (in warehouse location order) of the catalogue numbers of stock items that have changed.

Every Friday afternoon, a "Stock Order" Report is produced from the Stock File showing which items have to be ordered and the details of the supplier of that item. (This report is in Supplier Number order).

e. **Supplier and Price File Maintenance**. Supplier details and prices are changed as soon as they are announced by a supplier. Whenever prices are changed, a "Price Amendment" List is printed out and sent to all agents, by accessing the Agent File sequentially to obtain name and address details.

If items are added to or deleted from the Stock file, the corresponding operation is carried out on the Supplier and Price File.

c. ASSIGNMENT

1. List the possible contents of the three master files. (Include notes for each data item showing the reason for its inclusion). (12 marks)

2. Describe the controls that could be incorporated on a batch of orders. (Give an example by generating some order data and showing how your control procedure would work). (8 marks)

3. Describe the validation checks that could be performed on the order data. (8 marks)

4. Draw a *system* flowchart for each of the sub-systems a, b, c, d and e. (Annotate freely in order to explain exactly what takes place during any particular run). (45 marks)

5. Suggest the possible contents of the "Stock Order" Report, by showing the format of the printed report. (This should give the exact layout of all the data items in the report). (8 marks)

6. State the point at which, a check on the possibility of an agent exceeding his credit limit, might be carried out. Briefly describe the necessary changes in the design of the system, required by the inclusion of such a check.

(6 marks)

7. Describe the measures that could be taken in order to protect the files against loss or corruption. Distinguish clearly between the measures for files held on magnetic tape and those held on magnetic disc. (10 marks)

8. Suggest a way of checking on 'slow-moving' stock items ie those which have not been ordered for at least two years. (3 marks)

27

15 Telephone Invoicing System

a. DESCRIPTION

BACKGROUND

A computer-based system is used to handle the production of telephone bills for a local GPO Telephone Area. The system operates as follows.

On the 1st February, 1st May, 1st August and 1st November of each year all telephone customers receive a bill for the use of their telephones. Each of these bills will contain the following:–

Customer's name, address and telephone number.

Date of bill.

Telephone quarterly rental charge.

Previous and Current Meter Readings.

Number of dialled units used and their cost @ 5p per unit.

Description, date and cost of each miscellaneous service used, eg operator-connected calls, telegrams, reversed-charged calls etc.

Total of all above charges.

Value Added Tax @ 15 per cent of this total, and

Total payable (ie inclusive of VAT).

Prior to the production of these bills each customer's telephone meter is read. In order to evaluate the number of dialled units used, the previous reading (ie of three months ago) must be subtracted from the current reading.

Miscellaneous services used via the operator, ie not recorded automatically, must be recorded manually as and when they occur. The operator evaluates the cost of each service and records it on a Miscellaneous Calls Work Sheet.

Payments of bills are also recorded by the Accounts Section as and when they are paid. These are entered into the system every two weeks and a copy retained by the Accounts Section.

OUTLINE OF COMPUTER BASED SYSTEM

The data for each customer is held on three disc files, which are described below:

FILE 1: CUSTOMER FILE contains 1 record for each customer organised indexed sequentially in telephone number order. This data will not alter during a three month period, and includes:–

Telephone number.

Customer name.

Customer address line 1.

Customer address line 2.

Quarterly rental charge.

FILE 2: INVOICE FILE contains one record for each customer organised indexed sequentially in telephone number order of quarterly data, and includes:–

Telephone number.

Balance outstanding.

Last meter reading.

Dialled units used.

FILE 3: MISCELLANEOUS FILE contains one record for each miscellaneous service used since the last invoice run. There may be zero, one or many such services on the same or different dates for each customer. This file is organised sequentially in telephone number order, and includes:–

Telephone number.

Description of service.

Date of Service.

Cost of Service.

The overall system is comprised of a number of inter-related sub-systems, which are now described.

Every three months, meter-readings are used to update File 2 with the numbers of units used (ie difference of new reading and previous reading).

Every week, the previous weeks miscellaneous service data is merged in telephone number and date order onto File 3.

Every two weeks, payments are input in any order and the balance on File 2 is adjusted by accessing the file randomly.

Every three months a bill is printed for each customer in telephone number order by accessing all three files sequentially. When the total payable is calculated then the balance on File 2 is updated.

The system allows for new customers, changes of name, address and rental charge for existing customers and deletions of customers from File 1.

The system also allows for changes in the rate of VAT and cost of dialling.

b. FLOWCHARTING ASSIGNMENT

The assignment is to prepare a *system* flowchart for the overall system.

This is achieved by drawing up a system flowchart for each sub-system, showing clearly the required runs and how they relate to each other.

Furthermore the inter-relationships between the various sub-systems should be clearly marked, showing the flow of data between them.

The flowcharts should be annotated wherever necessary and clearly labelled eg each sub-system should have a clear title, file names should be clearly stated.

For each sub-system, decide on whether a transaction file should be sorted before updating a master file sequentially or whether to update the master file by accessing records directly.

c. DOCUMENTATION ASSIGNMENT

BACKGROUND

You are a systems analyst who has been given the task of designing a complete computer-based system to handle the production of telephone invoices for your local GPO telephone area (as described in 15 a.).

It is your task to produce full system documentation, which will be retained for future reference.

ASSIGNMENT

The complete assignment will consist of a written systems manual (of 20-30 pages), which will describe the complete working of the system.

It will contain the following sections.

1. Objects of the system. The objects of the system will be set out in a clear manner and any benefits which will accrue from the system should be specified.

2. System Description. A general description of the system will be given and will *clearly distinguish* between clerical and computer procedures.

3. System Flowchart. A flowchart of the complete system will be drawn up showing all the programs and files required. This will show how each program run relates to the others so that the flow of information between them complies with the requirements of the overall system.

4. Equipment required. A brief description of the equipment required to run the system will be given. You may also include: number of runs, frequency of runs (what is performed daily, weekly, monthly, etc.).

5. Input specification. This will contain details of the basic data required and the sources from which this is obtained.

30

6. Output specification. The following items will be included whenever they apply:

    a.   Output media.

    b.   Headings.

    c.   Report details.

    d.   Special forms.

7. File specification. The following items will be included:

    a.   Medium.

    b.   File names.

    c.   File layout and record description.

    d.   File protection.

8. Control. This section will specify the controls required on input/output and clearly allocate the responsibilities for same. Cut-off dates, priorities for the system, distribution of output and any other relevant information required for control will be given.

Part II

Programming Exercises

Introduction

Students, who are asked to specify, write and test programs, will be motivated by undertaking assignments to which they can relate and the purposes of which are evident. Also they require an exercise to which they can contribute some original thinking. From the lecturer's point of view, an assignment should give scope for an individual approach to a problem. This approach may be expressed in terms of the program structure, the method of calculation adopted or the format of the output report.

Data files have been used in the exercises wherever appropriate for two main reasons:

1. The student is given a practical introduction to the important concepts of files and records.

2. It facilitates comprehensive program testing, by allowing the creation of other data files on which to test the program. The student is thus made aware of the importance of the creation and use of suitable test data.

As the exercises have already been tried and tested, in some cases names are given to the data files. These files can initially be created on the student's computer system by the lecturer responsible, or the students may create their own data files.

In most cases the student will have access to a timesharing service on which he or she can develop and store both programs and data files. In fact the exercises were designed for this type of installation. However the exercises may just as easily be carried out on a micro-computer based configuration.

Exercises 1 and 2 are elementary examples using READ and DATA statements, in order to introduce the student to the concept of program loops and rogue values.

The program comprehension exercises following, give the student an opportunity to follow through a working program and to test their understanding of its actions.

Exercises 4, 5 and 6 are straightforward analyses and reporting on one data file using one loop. In each case an entity in the system has just one record.

Exercise 7 is an extension of the above type of program; it has a variable number of transaction records for each customer in the system.

(N.B. The above exercises do not require knowledge of FOR . . . NEXT statements, arrays or subroutines. These topics are dealt with in the next two problems. These problems use READ and DATA statements, and are examples of program loops controlled by FOR . . . NEXT statements)

Exercise 8 requires knowledge of FOR . . . NEXT statements and arrays. It is an open-ended exercise, giving scope for a variety of solutions.

Exercise 9 is a shorter exercise and tests the use of subroutines and arrays.

Exercise 10 analyses and reports on a file, but with the requirement of use of subroutines.

Finally Exercise 11 is the most demanding and time-consuming, but gives a practical insight into file updating, which is an important topic in data processing. It involves the use of three data files.

A summary of BASIC programming language statements is given in Appendix D.

1 Employee Pay Calculation

Write a BASIC program to read the following data about employees:

Employee Number, Employee Name, Number of Hours Worked, Hourly Rate of Pay (in £),

and to print a simplified payslip in a suitable format.

ASSUMPTIONS

i. The program is to use READ and DATA statements.
ii. Tax is to be deducted at the rate of 30% of Gross Pay.
iii. Data for about five employees is to be designed by the student.
iv. The end of data is to be signified by an Employee Number of –9999.

2 Customer Invoice Calculation

Write a BASIC program to read the following data concerning items sold to a customer:

Item Number, Item Description, Quantity Sold, Unit Price,

and to print out a simplified invoice, showing all items and total payable, in an appropriate format.

ASSUMPTIONS

i. The program is to use READ and DATA statements.
ii. VAT is to be charged at the rate of 15%.
iii. Data for about five items is to be designed by the student.
iv. The end of data is to be signified by an Item Number of – 9999.

3 Program Comprehension Exercises*

Note: The asterisk denotes that an answer to the exercise is to be found in Part IV.

a. EXAMINATION RESULTS ANALYSIS

The following BASIC program is used to process students' exam results. The program reads records from a data file named 'RESULT' and writes records onto two other data files named 'FILE 2' and 'FILE 3'.

Read through the program, then answer the questions that follow:

```
10   A$='(########      (########      (#########'
20   B$=' ###.#        ###.#        ###.#'
30   DEFINE READ FILE #1='RESULT'
40   ON END #1 GOTO 270
50   DEFINE FILE #2='FILE2'
60   DEFINE FILE #3='FILE3'
70   T1=0
80   T2=0
90   T3=0
100  N1=0
110  N2=0
120  READ #1,N$,A,E,S
130  T1=T1+A
140  T2=T2+E
150  T3=T3+S
160  M=(A+E+S)/3
170  IF M<45 THEN  GOTO 240
180  IF A<35 THEN  GOTO 240
190  IF E<35 THEN  GOTO 240
200  IF S<35 THEN  GOTO 240
210  WRITE #2,N$,A,E,S,M
220  N1=N1+1
230  GOTO 120
240  WRITE #3,N$,M
250  N2=N2+1
260  GOTO 120
270  PRINT
280  PRINT
290  PRINT USING A$,'ACCOUNTS','ECONOMICS','STATISTICS'
300  PRINT USING B$,T1/(N1+N2),T2/(N1+N2),T3/(N1+N2)
310  PRINT
320  PRINT
330  PRINT USING B$,N1/(N1+N2)*100,N2/(N1+N2)*100
340  CLOSE #1
350  CLOSE #2
360  CLOSE #3
370  END
```

38

a. State what the contents of FILE 2 and FILE 3 will be after the program has run.

b. What criteria are used to determine whether a students' data is written onto FILE 2 or onto FILE 3?

c. What information is printed out at line 300?

d. What information is printed out at line 330?

e. Design suitable test data which could be used in conjunction with this program to check that it is logically correct. Show the results that will be obtained with your test data.

b. DATA VALIDATION

A customer file consists of records holding customer number (four digits) and the amount of the payment made by the customer.

The following BASIC program is used (in this particular system) to check the validity of the customer number. The program reads records from a data file named 'CUST' and writes valid records onto another data file named 'VALID'. Invalid records are listed together with an error message eg ERROR TYPE X, where X can be 1, 2 or 3.

```
10    REM DATA VALIDATION PROGRAM
20    DEFINE READ FILE #1='CUST1'
30    DEFINE FILE #2='VALID'
40    REM C1 IS COUNT OF NUMBER OF RECORDS READ
50    C1=0
60    REM C2 IS COUNT OF NUMBER OF VALID RECORDS
70    C2=0
80    REM READ CUSTOMER RECORDS AND PERFORM VALIDATION CHECKS
90    READ #1,C,P
100   ON END #1 GOTO 9000
110   REM L IS SUBSCRIPT OF ERROR TYPE
120   L=1
130   C1=C1+1
140   IF C<0 THEN  GOTO 1010
150   L=2
160   IF C<1000 THEN  GOTO 1010
170   IF C>9999 THEN  GOTO 1010
180   L=3
190   IF C>4999 THEN  GOTO 210
200   GOTO 230
210   IF C<6000 THEN  GOTO 1010
220   REM RECORD IS VALID
230   C2=C2+1
240   WRITE #2,C,P
250   GOTO 90
1000  REM PRINTING OF APPROPRIATE ERROR MESSAGE
1010  PRINT '*********************************'
1020  PRINT ' ERROR MESSAGE FOR RECORD ':C1
1030  PRINT '  ERROR TYPE  ':L
```

```
1040    PRINT 'RECORD DETAILS ARE':C:P
1050    PRINT
1060    GOTO 90
9000    WRITE #2,C2
9010    PRINT 'DATA VALIDATION COMPLETED'
9020    CLOSE #1
9030    CLOSE #2
9040    END
```

a.   State the conditions that would generate the printing of each of the three error messages.

b.   Design test data which could be used in conjunction with the validation program to check all possible conditions of the data.

State clearly the output that each record of your test data will produce.

c.   How could the information, passed onto the 'VALID' file at line 9000 in the program, be used later.

d.   A modification to the program is required in order to detect a particular customer whose cheques will not be honoured.

Write the extra BASIC instructions (including line numbers) to input this customer number via the keyboard, and if that customer record is found in the file, then the message ERROR TYPE 4 should be printed.

The record should not be passed onto the 'VALID' file.

4 Job Placement

A job placement company keeps a file of unemployed qualified personnel, who are seeking employment.

Each record on the file consists of:

Name
Address
Telephone Number
Age
Profession
Highest Qualification
Final Salary (during last employment)
Required Salary

Draw a flowchart, write and run a BASIC program, which will read the file and print out the following:

a. The names and addresses of accountants, aged over 35 years and under 45 years, who are prepared to take a post at less than their previous salary.

b. The total number of accountants who are aged over 35 years and under 45 years.

41

5 Stock Re-Order Report*

A data file named 'STOCK' holds stock records, which contain the following items:

   a. Item Code (6 characters).

   b. Item Description (12 characters).

   c. Quantity in Stock.

   d. Re-order Quantity, Re-order Level.

   e. Supplier Name (12 characters).

   f. Supplier Address – First Line (12 characters).

   g. Supplier Address – Second Line (12 characters).

   h. Item Selling Price (in pounds).

Draw a flowchart, write and run a BASIC program, which will read the Stock File and print out:

   i. An order report for items with quantities below the re-order level. The report should include Supplier Name and Address, Item Code and Description, Quantity Ordered.

   ii. The number of different stock items ordered.

   iii. Sales value of all current stock.

The complete assignment will consist of:

   a. A flowchart of the program.

   b. A listing of the program.

   c. A RUN of the program which prints the re-order report, number of different items ordered and current stock sales value.

6 Gas Bill Preparation*

Construct a flowchart, write and run a BASIC program that will prepare Gas Bills for a number of customers.

The program will obtain the data for the customers by reading from a file called GASCST. The data for each customer will be as follows:–

a. Customer Name

b. Customer Account Number (seven digits)

c. Customer Address

d. Customer Town or City

e. Post Code

f. Quarterly Standing Charge (in pounds)

g. Previous Meter Reading (six digits)

h. Current Meter Reading (six digits)

The program must calculate the units used and then the corresponding charge may be worked out by multiplying the units used by the required cost per unit. The program reads the cost per unit from a file called GASDAT, which holds the following data:–

a. 1st Field is the Cost (in pence) per Unit used (for the first 250 units).

b. 2nd Field is the Cost (in pence) per Unit used (for all subsequent units over 250).

The program must print a Gas Bill for each customer showing, at least, the customer's name and address, account number, number of units used, cost per unit and Total charge. (PRINTUSING statements may be used to obtain a neat layout).

NOTE: Some customer's data may have been incorrectly entered on the file. Therefore the program must include a check on the validity of data (in this exercise, the value of the Standing Charge cannot be greater than £12.49, and the meter readings must be positive six digit numbers). If a record has any invalid data, a Gas Bill should *not* be prepared, but an appropriate message should be printed out.

The complete assignment will consist of:

a. A flowchart of the program

b. A listing of the program (which should be annotated with REM statements).

c. A RUN of the program which prints the Gas Bills.

7 Credit Card Statement Preparation*

Construct a flowchart, write and run a BASIC program that will prepare statements for a credit card company's customers.

The program will obtain data for the customers by reading from a file called CARDAT. The data for each customer will be as follows:–

a. Customer's name.

b. Previous outstanding balance.

c. Payment received since last statement.

d. Date of statement, in the form:– Day, Month, Year (eg 8, DEC, 80).

e. A number of transactions, which consist of:–
   i.   Date of Transaction in the form:– Day, Month, Year.
   ii. Name of outlet, where transaction took place.
   iii. Amount of Transaction.

The last transaction for a customer will contain only 99,XXX,99 in the date field.

The program must print a statement for each customer, showing at least, the customer's name, date of statement, previous outstanding balance, payment received since last statement, opening balance for this month, each transaction and the final balance.

If the opening balance for this month is greater than zero, an interest charge of 2½% of the opening balance is added.

The last record on the file will be as follows:–

a. First field will contain LAST.

b. 2nd field will be the number of customers on the file.

c. 3rd field will be the number of transactions on the file.

d. 4th field will be the total of the previous outstanding balances on the file.

e. 5th field will be the total of the transactions on the file.

When the program has printed the last statement, it must then print a report showing the values read from the last record and the equivalent values calculated by the program whilst it is reading the file.

(N.B. Ensure that the program will report if any calculated and read values are in disagreement).

The complete assignment will consist of:–

a. A flowchart of the program.

b. A listing of the program, which should be annotated with REM statements.

c. A RUN of the program which prints the Statements and the control report.

NOTE: Data file and output listing only shown in solution.

8 Company Sales Report*

BACKGROUND
A company bottling and selling soft drinks has a head office in London and 50 branch offices throughout the United Kingdom. A recent graduate in economics has been appointed to the Head Office Planning Team. His first task is to write a BASIC program, which will be used to accept the last three year's sales data for a branch, carry out a suitable analysis and output the results in a form suitable for the company's board of directors.

As an example, the figures for branch 1 are given below.

	Year 1		Year 2		Year 3
Month	Sales, (1,000 standard bottles)	Month	Sales	Month	Sales
1	199.0	1	287.0	1	300.0
2	211.0	2	291.0	2	310.0
3	210.0	3	294.0	3	305.0
4	224.0	4	299.0	4	340.0
5	220.0	5	299.0	5	348.0
6	210.0	6	301.0	6	335.0
7	200.0	7	280.0	7	295.0
8	145.0	8	190.0	8	250.0
9	130.0	9	160.0	9	210.0
10	121.0	10	171.0	10	180.0
11	119.0	11	162.0	11	200.0
12	120.0	12	178.0	12	205.0

ASSIGNMENT
1. To decide on a suitable way in which the sales figures could be analysed and compared eg for each year you might calculate monthly high/low, mean etc. (The final decision on data analysis is left entirely up to you, but marks will be awarded for originality and clear presentation of output).

2. To construct a flowchart and write a BASIC program, which carries out your chosen analysis and outputs the results in a form suitable for top management eg you might feel a diagram showing the input data in graphical form could be included in the output.

3. RUN the program using the data for branch 1.

4. Produce:–

a. a listing of the program (which should be annotated with REM statements);

b. a flowchart of the program;

c. a RUN of the program, which prints the analysis of Branch 1's figures.

NOTE: The output listing only is shown in the solution.

9 Aptitude Test Marking

Ten job candidates take an aptitude test, which consists of ten questions, each possible answer being 1, 2 or 3.

Construct a flowchart and write a BASIC program to do the following:

1. Read in the correct results and store them in array A eg

$$A(1) = 2, \quad A(2) = 3, \quad A(3) = 3, \quad \text{etc.}$$

2. Read in the ten candidates' results and store them in array X eg

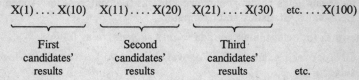

X(1).... X(10)   X(11).... X(20)   X(21).... X(30)   etc.... X(100)

    First   Second   Third
candidates'   candidates'   candidates'
  results   results   results   etc.

3. Call a subroutine which evaluates the score for each candidate in array S eg

$$S(1) = \text{score of candidate 1}$$
$$S(2) = \text{score of candidate 2}$$
$$\text{etc.}$$

(This is done by comparing each candidates' answers with the correct answers stored in array A and allocating one mark for each correct answer).

4. Output the number of the candidate with the highest score and an appropriate message.

10 Student Marks*

Construct a flowchart, write and run a BASIC program, which will analyse student exam and coursework marks in order to print a pass list and an overall summary report.

The program reads data from a file named 'MARKS', which holds records consisting of:–

a. Student Number.

b. Student Name.

c. Four fields holding exam marks (percentages) for: Accounts, Economics, Statistics and Computing.

d. Four fields holding coursework marks (percentages) for: Accounts, Economics, Statistics and Computing.

The rules for determining a grade *in any subject* are as follows:–

70% or over in exam and 70% or over in coursework is a distinction in that subject,

55% or over in exam and 55% or over in coursework is a credit in that subject,

40% or over in exam and 40% or over in coursework is a pass in that subject, otherwise a fail in the subject.

The rules for determining an overall result *for the course* are as follows:–

Combined exam marks and coursework marks over 350 then 'PROCEED' to next year of course, otherwise 'REPEAT' the year (any failed subjects will have to be re-sit).

The program should print two reports:

    i.   a pass list showing all subject marks and grades for each student, together with overall result;

    ii.   a summary report eg average mark for each subject, pass rate in each subject etc.

The complete assignment will consist of:

a. A flowchart of the program *(not shown in the solution)*.

b. A listing of the program (which should be annotated with REM statements).

c. A RUN of the program which prints the two reports.

11 Mailing List Update

Construct a flowchart, write and run a BASIC program that will update a Mailing List File (MAIL) by means of adjustments contained in a Transaction File (TRANS), in order to produce an updated Mailing List File (select a name of your choice).

THE CUSTOMER MASTER FILE (MAIL) contains one record for each customer, set out as follows:

Line 1: Customer Number, Customer Name

Line 2: Street, Town, County

Line 3: Postal Code, Telephone Exchange and Number

the last record contains two lines only, set out as follows:–

Line 1: 9999, END

Line 2: Total number of Customers on File.

THE TRANSACTION FILE (TRANS) contains 3 types of record set out as follows:–

a. *Addition records.* These records will be used to add the details of new customers to the Mailing List File. Each addition record will deal with one customer only and is set out in 4 lines as follows:–

Line 1: Customer Number, ADD

Line 2: Customer Name, Street

Line 3: Town, County, Postal Code

Line 4: Telephone Exchange and Number.

b. *Deletion records.* These records will be used to remove details of customers from the Mailing List File. Each record removes one customer only and consists of one line only, set out as follows:–

Line 1: Customer Number, DEL

c. *Modify records.* These records will be used to change the contents of a particular field in a customer's record on the Updated Mailing List. Each record modifies one field in one customer's record only and is set out in 2 lines as follows:–

Line 1: Customer Number, MOD

Line 2: Name of field to be modified, New value of field to be modified.

In Line 2 the Name of field to be modified may take only the following four-character values.

NAME, STRT, TOWN, CNTY, POST, TELE.

There may be up to five modify records for any one customer record.

The last record on the Transaction file consists of 2 lines set out as follows:—

Line 1: 9999, END

Line 2: Number of Addition Records, Number of Deletion Records, Number of Modify records.

the Updated Mailing List must have records in the same format as the original List.

(N.B. Records on all the files will be in strict ascending order of Customer Numbers).

At the end of the run the program must print out a control report showing the old values of the control totals, the transaction values and the new values.

The complete assignment will consist of:—

a. A summary flowchart of the program.

b. A listing of the program (which should be annotated with REM statements).

c. A RUN of the program, which prints the control report.

d. A listing of the updated Mailing List.

Part III

Solutions to Systems Exercises 1-8

1 Company Application Areas

Company Type	Business Area	Computer Reports
a. **National Airline**	Operations	Timetables Aircraft Schedules Crew Schedules Aircraft Maintenance Reports Aircraft History Reports Operating Costs
	Finance	Profit/Loss Analysis Management Reports Payroll Supplier Payments Agents' Commission
	Sales	Seat Reservations Payment Details Agent Details
	Freight Carriage	Freight Schedules Freight Costing Details Customer Listings
	Purchasing	Supplier Details
b. **Food Manufacturer**	Production	Production Schedules Production Costs
	Stock Control	Current Stock Lists Stock on order Demand Forecasts Re-order Lists
	Sales	Sales Ledger Analysis Sales Forecasts Sales History Customer Listing
	Marketing	Customer Type Analysis Sales Breakdown Analysis
	Purchasing	Purchase Ledger Analysis Supplier Listing

	Finance	General Ledger Analysis
		Balance Sheet
		Payroll
		VAT Reporting

c. **Local Authority**

	Rate Accounting	Rate Demands
		Rateable Value Lists
		Management Summary Reports
	Housing	Housing Lists
		Maintenance Schedules
		Housing Rent Reports
	Planning	Planning Applications
		Project Control Schedules
		(ie Critical Path Analysis)
		for new building projects.
		Traffic Surveys.
	Property Register	Authority Property List
		Compulsory Purchase Orders
		Building Inspections
	Highway, Transport & Waste Disposal	Highways Maintenance Schedules
		Authority Vehicle Lists
		Vehicle Mileage and Petrol Consumption Details.
	Education	Pupil Rolls
		Staff Lists
		School Lists
	Electoral Register	List of Electors
	Finance	Accounts Payable Details
		Report of Loans Made to Authority
		Mortgages Lent by Authority.

d. **National Magazine Publisher**

	Sales and Distribution	Customer Sales Figures
		Sales Analysis
	Marketing	Client Sales Figures
		Advertising Reservations
	Printing	Printing Schedules
		Printing Costs

54

Raw Material	Supplier Details
Purchasing	Cost Figures
Finance	Customer Account Status
	Invoice from Suppliers
	Payments to Suppliers
	Invoices to Customers
	Payments from Customers
	Invoices to Clients
	Payments from Clients
	Outstanding Debts
	Management Reports
	Payroll
	VAT Reporting

(N.B. The term "customers" is used to denote wholesalers who purchase and sell publisher's output.
The term "client" is used for organisations who purchase advertising space).

e.	**Estate Agent**	Customer Liaison	Mailing Lists
		Housing	Sellers and Housing Details
		Building Society Liaison	Society Loan Facilities
		Finance	Invoice to Customers/Solicitors
			Payments from Customers
			Outstanding Debt Reports
			VAT Reporting

2 Types of DP Files

a. PAYROLL SYSTEM

i. **Employee File:**

Employee Reference Number – *Record Key*
Sex,
First Names,
Last Name,
Date of Birth,
Staff Grade,
National Insurance Number,
National Insurance Code,
Income Tax Code
Date Started,
Date Left,
Basic Annual Salary,
Pension fund contributions,
Employers National Insurance Contributions,
Employees National Insurance Contributions,
Gross Pay to Date,
Gross Tax to Date,
Bank Account Number,
Bank and branch sorting code,
Bank Name and Address;
(Master File)

ii. **Employee Changes File;**

Employee Reference Number – *Record Key*
Changes Code eg Starter, Leaver or Modification,
Details according to type of change;
(Transaction File)

iii. **Employee Hours Worked File;**

Employee Reference Number – *Record Key*
Number of Normal Hours Worked,
Number of Overtime Hours Worked,
Overtime Rate;
(Transaction File)

iv. **Reference File;**

National Insurance Codes and corresponding Deductions
Staff Grades and corresponding rate of pension fund deductions.

(Common Data File)

Batch Processing Operations would be used throughout the system.

b. MAIL ORDER SYSTEM

   i. **Order File;**

Order Number – *Record Key*
Agent Number,
Stock Item Code,
Quantity ordered,
Total Price;
(Transaction File)

   ii. **Stock File;**

Stock Item Code – *Record Key*
Item Description,
Quantity in Stock,
Supplier Details,
Price,
Re-order Level,
Re-order Quantity;
(Master File)

   iii. **Agent File;**

Agent Number – *Record Key*
Agent Name and Address
Credit Limit
Summary of Previous Transactions
Commission details;
(Master File)

   iv. **Ordered Items File:**

Invoice Number – *Record Key*
Order Number,
Agent Number,
Stock Item Codes, Description and Prices,
Invoice Total;
(Working File)

   v. **Stock Changes File:**

Stock Item Code – *Record Key*
Changes Code eg Addition, Deletion or Modification
Details according to type of change;
(Transaction File)

    vi. **Stock Receipts File:**

Stock Item Code – *Record Key*
Quantity Received;

(Transaction File)

    vii. **Agent Changes File:**

Agent Number – *Record Key*
Changes Code eg Addition, Deletion or Modification
Details according to type of change;

(Transaction File)

Batch processing operations would be used.

c. STOLEN CAR SYSTEM

Stolen Car File;

Car Registration Number – *Record Key*
Make and Model
Date reported stolen
Reference to Police Station, where theft reported.
Place stolen;

(Master File)

Car Changes File;

Car Registration Number – *Record Key*
Changes Code eg Add to or delete from file;

(Transaction File)

On-line terminal enquiries would be made of the system, and owner details would be kept at police station, where theft was reported.

Cars which have remained on file for a certain period of time would have their records removed and archived.

d. COMPUTER DATING SYSTEM

    i. **Male Attributes File;**

Agency Code Number – *Record Key*
Name and Address,
Age Group (Date of Birth)
Personal Details.
List of Interests;

(Master File)

ii. **Female Requirements File;**

Agency Code Number – *Record Key*
Name and Address,
Required attributes, interests;
(Transaction File)

The Female Requirements File may be matched against the Male Attribute File in order to find the closest match(es). The system would also require a Female Attributes File and Male Requirements File. Alternatively a single Master File could be used and processed by different programs, depending on whether the run is to find females for males or vice versa.

e. SHIPPING COMPANY SYSTEM

i. **Ship File:**

Ship Registration Number – *Record Key*
Ship Name
Owner,
Registered Port,
Ship Details eg length, cargo space, type
Present Captain Details eg name, registration number
Crew details,
Trip details eg ports of call, estimated dates of arrival;
(Master File)

ii. **Cargo File;**

Company's Cargo Number – *Record Key*
Cargo Description,
Cargo Owners,
Insurance Value,
Loading Point,
Destination Port,
Company Charge;
(Master File)

iii. **Port Reference File;**

Port Name – *Record Key*
Country,
Harbour Fees,
Name, Address, Telephone Number of local representative;
(Master File)

3 Job Functions of a Systems Analyst

The following is a selection of job functions from a number of different adverts.

Advert 1. **Systems Analyst for engineering company**

"ability to liaise effectively with user departments in order to establish new project specifications";

"to provide full back-up documentation and user training for existing systems"

Advert 2. **Systems Analyst for Management Services Division of a nationalised industry.**

"to assess the feasibility of new systems and see them through to implementation"

"to maintain and update new systems"

"to determine priorities on both a long and short term basis"

Advert 3. **Systems Analyst for financial environment**

"to increase the scope of overall support in the fields of finance and administration"

"to evaluate existing systems"

"to prepare outline and detailed systems specifications and the subsequent development of these through to implementation"

Advert 4. **Systems Analyst for manufacturing company**

"to work on the development and subsequent amendments of computer based systems"

"to develop an important phase of the company's costing system"

Advert 5. **Systems Analyst for multi-national engineering organisation**

"to be a member of a small corporate team providing expertise in evaluating the effectiveness and integrity of current systems, undertaking reviews of existing management controls and operations, and commenting on the viability of future computer systems".

SUMMARY AND CONCLUSIONS OF PREVIOUS WORK EXPERIENCE

The previous work experience required will be dependent on the particular company's requirements at the time of advertising, and is likely to fall into one of the following areas:

previous systems analysis experience

There may be a requirement for knowledge of a particular area eg banking, retailing etc.

There may be a requirement for previous use of a particular software package or database management system.

previous programming experience

There may be a need for the analyst to be fully conversant with the main programming language used by the company.

previous organisation and methods experience

There may be a need for an O & M analyst, who is used to adopting a systematic approach to problems. This would be important when the vacant position was more in the nature of business analyst rather than computer analyst. It might also be useful to employ an O & M analyst either from within the same or similar company and then train him in systems analysis and design techniques.

new entrants to systems work

There are times when a company invites applications from people with no previous experience in this field, eg fresh graduates, company staff working outside the Data Processing Department.

In each case the number of years experience required will depend on the level of staff, that the company is seeking.

4 Computerisation Studies

a. HOTEL

a. Benefits

i. Clients' accounts will be accurate and complete at any given time.

ii. Reduction in loss of services data eg loss of client signed ticket before reaching accounts desk.

iii. Items on the bill may be deleted and the bill re-calculated more quickly than before.

iv. Facilitates changes in room number, accommodation rate.

v. Reduce staff fiddling (client gets receipt of each service).

vi. Reduction in processing cost.

vii. Analysis of use and profitability of each area of operation and service.

viii. Monthly or weekly cash flow statements may be provided.

b. Stages. Investigation, Analysis, Design, Programming, System Testing, Documentation, Maintenance, Review.

c. Problems

i. System vulnerable to hardware failure

- all updating might be carried out on two duplicate master files

- a second cpu may be necessary as a stand-by.

ii. System may have loss of data during transmission

- daily reconciliation check : total no. of transactions from all terminals = total no. of master file amendments.

iii. Invalid data may be entered

- validation check for inconsistency eg no hair cuts in restaurants

- range check for maximum and minimum values eg no negative entries.

iv. Incorrect room number given – check with name or hotel key at time of data entry.

d. Future Application Areas

Future Reservations/Cancellations

Room occupancy statistics

Room availability reports

Hotel staff payroll

Stock control

Ordering of supplies
Payment of suppliers
Hotel Maintenance : building, repairs, servicing, replacement.
Preparation of menus

b. SUPERMARKET

i.   **Benefits**. The benefits to the supermarket may be classified into customer service and operational improvements.

This will lead to overall reductions in operating costs, more customer goodwill and an improved public image of a modern store. The benefits are now described.

Customer Service

1.   Customers will be charged accurately, as the prices of items may be stored on a central disc file and can be changed very quickly. This overcomes problems associated with missing price labels and assistants ringing up the wrong amounts.

2.   Customers may receive more informative bills with abbreviated descriptions of the items purchased.

3.   Customers should be serviced more quickly at the check-out terminals.

4.   Detection of fraud eg automatic check of lost or stolen credit cards.

5.   Potential for future introduction of electronic fund transfer (EFT) systems, linking terminals directly to customers' banks.

Operational Improvements

1.   Improved stock control eg latest stock situation available to management, automatic ordering.

2.   Improved utilisation of shelf space ie identification of fast and slow moving items.

3.   Improved management information eg daily terminal sales analysis, seasonal trends etc.

4.   Fewer staff may be required to operate the store.

ii.   **Implementation Plan**. The supermarket is likely to select one store in which to implement the system and examine the problems encountered, before introducing such a scheme into its other stores.

Activities necessary for system implementation

1. Feasibility Study/Hardware Selection/Visits to other installations.

2. Ordering and Awaiting Hardware Delivery.

3. Employment of Computer Staff.

4. Introduction of bar-coded labels and prices on shelves.

5. Staff Training eg Formal presentations, practical training. (This would be an on-going activity throughout the implementation phase).

6. Installation of Hardware.

7. Systems Development (eg implementing software packages, file creation).

8. System Testing.

9. Publicity Campaign (optional).

10. Live Running.

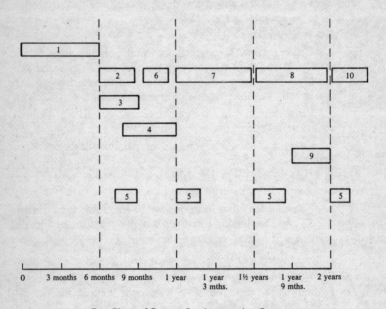

Bar Chart of System Implementation Stages

iii. Likely effects on supermarket staff

1. Union negotiations would need to discuss staff re-training, staffing level cuts, pay structures etc.

2. Initially there may be a decline in staff morale due to changes in the nature of the work, but this may change as job satisfaction should be increased.

3. Staff may decide to leave the store, in order to continue working with manual systems, for emotional reasons.

iv. **Potential operational problems**

1. Computer system may go down and therefore back-up facilities are essential.

2. Wrong price data may be entered and customers incorrectly charged.

3. Laser reading device may prove faulty causing delays at check-out counters.

4. New type of fraudulent practice may arise.

5 Introductory System Flowchart Exercises

a. MATCHING SITUATIONS WITH SYMBOLS

Flowchart
number

A Building Society counter clerk requests customers details via a teletype terminal.

9

A supermarket manager's orders (held on an OMR document) are input into a computer system

4

An Employee File (held on magnetic tape) is sorted into Employee Number order

3

Stock transactions (held on magnetic tape) are used to update a Stock Master File (also held on magnetic tape)

10

A credit card company's transactions are converted to microfilm prior to being processed via a key-to-tape machine

8

Data from a payroll calculation is output onto a disc for later printing of payslips

7

Clock cards are converted to punched cards

2

Payments (held on magnetic tape) are used to update a Sales Ledger (held on magnetic disc)

5

Orders are input and validated using a key-to-disc system, which writes the valid data to magnetic tape and prints an invalid order report

1

A message is output via the operator's console to indicate the the completion of the weekly sales analysis.

6

b. EMPLOYEE REPORTING

i. Complete employee
file listing

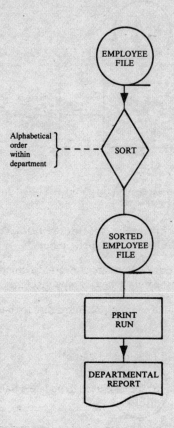

ii. Selected employee listing

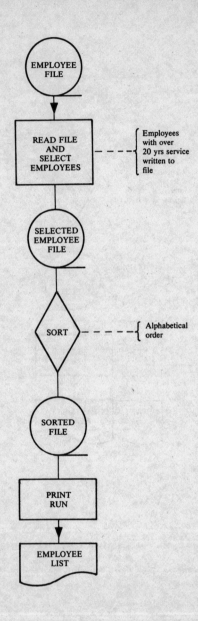

iii. Departmental
Report of average
years of service

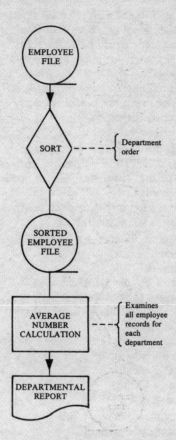

c. ELECTRICITY INVOICING COMPREHENSION

a. Source document eg meter reading sheet giving details of customer account number and present meter reading.

b. i. Keyboard input used for keying and verifying data.
ii. Batching of documents and creation of control totals.
iii. Correction of data input errors.

c. i. Incorrect customer account number.
    ii. Invalid meter reading eg insufficient digits, alpha characters used.
    iii. Incorrect batch totals.

d. If incorrect batch totals, then refer to original control record; or if validation error, then identify wrong data from Error Report. In both cases, the following steps would be undertaken:
    Locate original source document for the invalid record.
    Decision on whether:–
    – a data preparation error has been made or
    – the source document has been incorrectly completed.
    Make the required correction.
    Re-input the source document.

e. Meter readings are originally input in random sequence.
    The Customer Master File is held in account number sequence, hence a sort of the "Readings" file is necessary for subsequent matching of records.
    The file will be sorted into customer account number sequence (ie the same sequence as the master file).

f. Customer Account Number
    Customer Name
    Customer Address
    Tariff Type (eg Commercial, Domestic)
    Servicing payment (eg central heating)
    Budget payment (eg regular monthly payment)
    Total budget payment to date
    Electricity shop payment (eg appliances bought from local showroom)
    Total shop payment to date
    Previous Meter Reading
    Previous Balance Owing
    Date of last payment.

g. Standing Charge for different tariffs
    Cost per unit for different tariffs
    Any other standard information

h. 5 - Common Data or Reference File; 6 - Transaction File

i. i. keep the last master file and the last transaction file (grandfather-father-son principle)
    ii. make a duplicate copy of master files.
    iii. archive one file copy per month.

j. i. Control Report in order to check on satisfactory processing (eg all records processed correctly)
    ii. Error Report (eg mismatch of records between transactions and master files, duplicate records etc.)
    iii. Management Summary Report (eg Amounts owing by tariff types).

d. PRODUCTION CONTROL

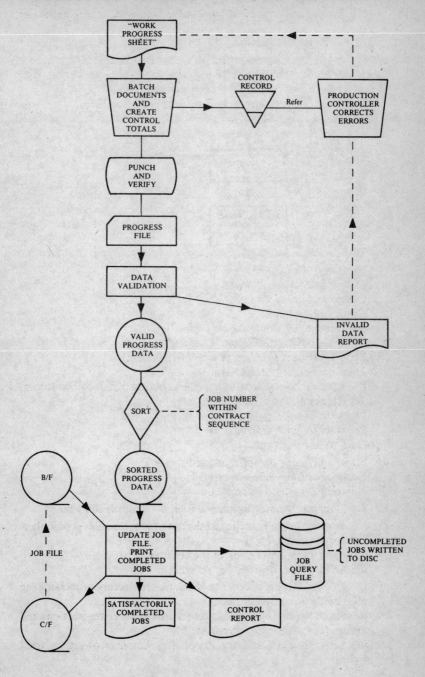

Production Control continuation

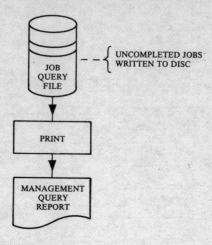

JOB
QUERY
FILE

--- { UNCOMPLETED JOBS
WRITTEN TO DISC

PRINT

MANAGEMENT
QUERY
REPORT

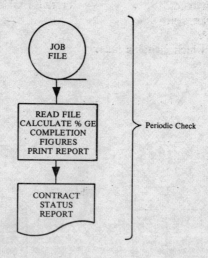

JOB
FILE

READ FILE
CALCULATE % GE
COMPLETION
FIGURES
PRINT REPORT

} Periodic Check

CONTRACT
STATUS
REPORT

6 Office Cleaning Firm

a. CLIENT MASTER FILE

Client No.

Site   Name & Address _____
                        _____
                        _____

Invoice Name & Address
         _____
         _____
         _____

Frequency of job   Floor Area
Price of job   Type of cleaning
Credit Limit   Special arrangements (coded)
Current Credit   Contract Starting date
Date of last payment   Contract Finishing date
Date last invoice sent
Date of last job
Hours during which cleaning must
be completed

b. i. UPDATE CLIENT FILE RUN (Irregular)

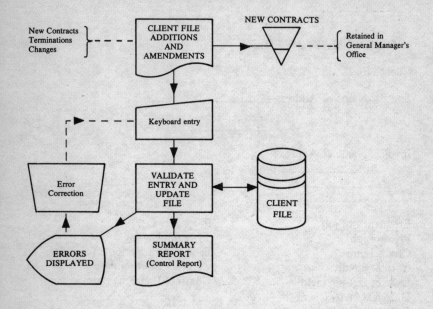

b. i. PAYMENT RUN (Irregular)

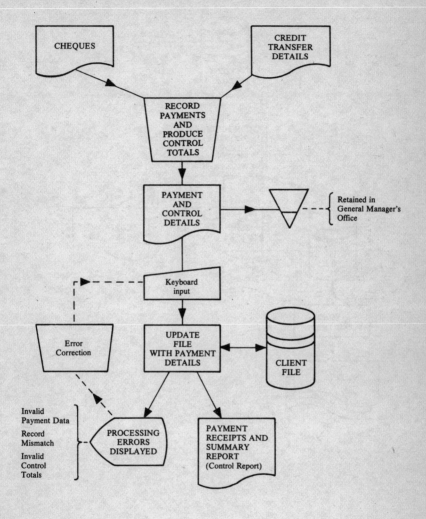

b. ii. PRINT RUN (Every Four weeks)

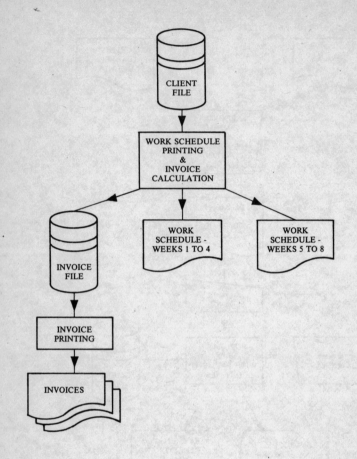

c. INTRODUCTION OF STAFFING DETAILS

A Staff Master File will have to be created, containing:
 Staff No.
 Name & Address
 Sex
 Age
 Job Function
 Banking details
 Employment details ie Tax Code, Salary to date etc etc.
 Wage Rate
 Hours in the day for which staff available
This could be used for following purposes:
 – Introduction of computerised payroll system.
 – Staff Allocation ie computerised allocation of staff to jobs.

77

7 Property Company System

The following mini-computer configuration would be appropriate for the property company:
- central processor unit
- two visual display units
- lineprinter
- two magnetic disc drives

a. CLIENT MASTER FILE:

Client Number
Client Name and Address
Invoice Name and Address
Office Address
Rateable Value
Floor Area
Floor level in building
Tenancy Type (eg leasehold)
Lease details

Contract Start date
Length of Contract
Monthly payment
Date of last payment
Amount of last payment
Payment to date (Current Year)
Date last invoice sent
Outstanding Balance

b. SUGGESTED STORAGE DEVICE

Magnetic Disc. The nature of the transactions (ie the client payments and file amendments, which will both take place throughout the year) means that they will be conveniently handled by the direct access facilities provided by discs.

c. SYSTEM FLOWCHART

1. Payment Input and Update Run

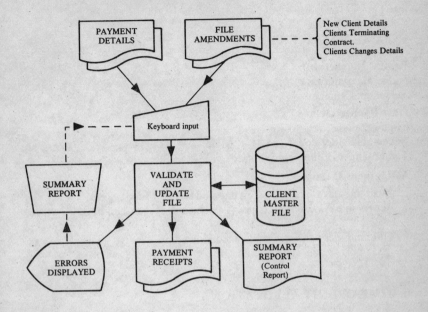

2. Invoice Print Run

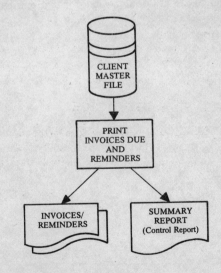

8 Babysitter System

a. FAMILY MASTER FILE

Family Number
Name and Address
Telephone Number

Host Family Details
Child details
Acceptable sitter codes (eg M = Male, T = Teenager)
Total number of time-credits used

Assignment Details
Available days and times (eg day codes 1 = Monday, etc)
Acceptable Assignment codes (eg babies < 1 year, children < 3 years, etc)
Total number of time-credits accumulated.

b. TIME CREDIT ALLOCATION

Every weekday hour up to midnight has a weighting of 1.
Every weekend hour up to midnight has a weighting of 1½.
Hours over midnight are at "double-rate" for that particular day.

c. SYSTEM FLOWCHART

1. Booking Request Run

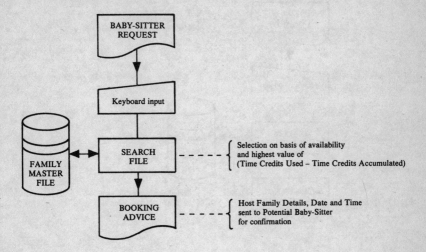

2. Time-Credit Update Run

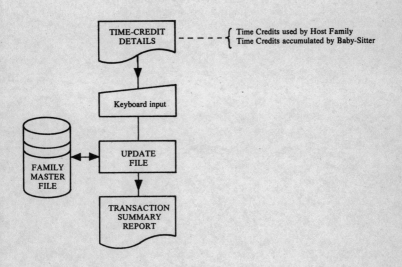

3. File Update Run

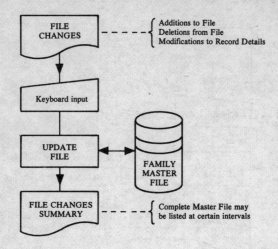

FILE
CHANGES ---- Additions to File
Deletions from File
Modifications to Record Details

Keyboard input

UPDATE
FILE ↔ FAMILY
MASTER
FILE

FILE CHANGES
SUMMARY ---- Complete Master File may
be listed at certain intervals

Part IV

Solutions to Selected Programming Exercises

INTRODUCTION

Full solutions are given to exercises 3, 5 and 6, in order to indicate the type and level of answer required.

In order that the other exercises may be used as class assignments, only part or even no answers are made available. In the case of part answers, these usually take the form of a listing of the particular data file used and an output listing of a program run using that data file. This gives students a target to aim for, while allowing them to develop their own individual programs.

The following table shows, for each question, the parts of the solution presented in this section.

EXERCISE NO.	Program Flowchart	Program Listing	Data File Listing	Output Listing
1 and 2	–	–	–	–
3 a. and b.	Complete solution to comprehension exercises is given			
4	–	–	–	–
5	*	*	*	*
6	*	*	*	*
7	–	–	*	*
8	–	–	given in question	*
9	–	–	–	–
10	–	*	*	*
11	–	–	–	–

Key: – not given in this section
* given in this section

85

3 Program Comprehension Exercises

a. EXAMINATION RESULTS ANALYSIS

a. FILE 2 contains records of students who have passed the examination and consists of the student's Name, the Accounts, Economics and Statistics marks, terminating with the average mark.

FILE 3 contains records of students who have failed the examination and consists of the student's Name and the average mark.

b. The conditions for a pass result are as follows:

No mark in any of the three subjects of Accounts, Economics and Statistics, can be below 35 AND the average mark cannot be less than 45.

c. The average mark (for all students) in the three subjects, Accounts, Economics and Statistics.

d. The percentage of students who passed and the percentage of students who failed.

e. 'Result' File (Test Data):

$$\text{G JONES, 86, 45, 47}$$
$$\text{F HALL, 56, 60, 54}$$
$$\text{K L TAYLOR, 68, 75, 74}$$
$$\text{P LAING, 40, 32, 50}$$

Program Run Output

ACCOUNTS	ECONOMICS	STATISTICS
62.5	53.0	56.3

75.0	25.0	

File 2 Contents:

G JONES	86	45	47	59.33
F HALL	56	60	54	56.67
K L TAYLOR	68	75	74	72.33

File 3 Contents:

P LAING	40.67

b. DATA VALIDATION

a. Error Type 1
     For Negative numbers.
     Error Type 2
     For numbers which are not 4 digits or have alphabetic characters.
     Error Type 3
     Any number commencing with 5

b. TEST DATA

Customer Number	Payment	
–4516,	14.00	Negative Number
212,	15.50	Less than 4 digits
15214,	18.43	More than 4 digits
3142,	17.50	Valid (under 5000)
5214,	13.42	Starts with a 5
6132,	17.00	Valid (over 5999)
ABCD,	15.00	Not a 4 digit Number

c. When the 'VALID' data file is processed, this number can be used as a control check.

d. 35   PRINT 'WHAT IS SUSPECT CUST NO'
     36   INPUT D
     135 IF C <> D THEN GOTO 140
     136 L = 4
     137 GOTO 1010

87

5 Stock Re-Order Report

RE-ORDER REPORT PROGRAM FLOWCHART

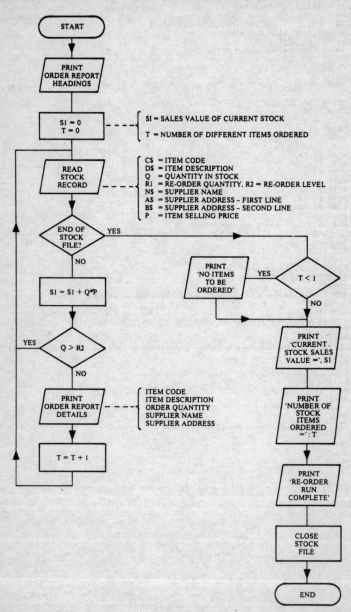

RE-ORDER REPORT PROGRAM LISTING

```
10   REM  PROGRAMMING EXERCISE NO. 5
20   REM  STOCK RE-ORDER REPORT
30   X$='  <#####    <###########    ###    <###########      <###########'
40   Y$='                                                      <###########'
50   Z$='          <###############################       ######. ##'
60   DEFINE READ FILE #1='STOCK'
70   ON END #1 GOTO 370
80   PRINT TAB(30):'RE-ORDER REPORT'
90   PRINT TAB(30):'======== ======'
100  PRINT
110  PRINT
120  PRINT TAB(3):'ITEM        ITEM        ORDER     SUPPLIER           SUPPLIER
130  PRINT TAB(3):'CODE        DESCRIPTION QUANTITY  NAME               ADDRESS'
140  PRINT TAB(3):'----        ----------- --------  --------           --------
150  PRINT
160  S1=0
170  T=0
180  READ #1,C$
190  READ #1,D$
200  READ #1,Q
210  READ #1,R1,R2
220  READ #1,N$
230  READ #1,A$
240  READ #1,B$
250  READ #1,P
260  REM  S1=SALES VALUE OF CURRENT STOCK
270  S1=S1+Q*P
280  IF Q>R2 THEN  GOTO 180
290  REM ITEM TO BE INCLUDED IN RE-ORDER REPORT
300  PRINT
310  PRINT USING X$,C$,D$,R1,N$,A$
320  PRINT USING Y$,B$
330  PRINT
340  REM T IS RUNNING TOTAL OF DIFFERENT STOCK ITEMS ORDERED
350  T=T+1
360  GOTO 180
370  IF T<1 THEN  PRINT ' *** NO ITEMS TO BE ORDERED ***'
380  PRINT
390  PRINT
400  PRINT '*******************************************************************'
410  PRINT
420  PRINT
430  PRINT USING Z$,'CURRENT STOCK SALES VALUE =',S1
440  PRINT
450  PRINT TAB(10):'NUMBER OF DIFFERENT STOCK ITEMS ORDERED = ':T
460  PRINT
470  PRINT
480  PRINT
490  PRINT '   *** RE-ORDER RUN COMPLETED ***'
500  CLOSE #1
510  END
```

89

RE-ORDER REPORT DATA FILE - STOCK

```
A11235                  C45010
BATH SCALES             SHOWER SPRAY
520                     32
800,100                 150,50
GRIMSHAWS               CASSELL LTD
12 PARK LANE            100 LEWES RD
LONDON W1               PORTSMOUTH
17.95                   15.00
A11236                  C56110
BATH CABINET            HEATED RAIL
24                      30
750,50                  100,30
GRIMSHAWS               PARKERS
12 PARK LANE            CROWN HOUSE
LONDON W1               MORDEN
35.00                   37.50
A11238                  C56125
TABLE LAMP              SHOWER BASE
0                       86
100,10                  100,50
VOLTAMP LTD             GRIMSHAWS
38 GREEN STR            12 PARK LANE
BIRMINGHAM 5            LONDON W1
7.50                    13.55
B22340
BABY COT
94
150,50
MOTHERY LTD
THE SQUARE
GRIMSBY
36.00
```

RE-ORDER REPORT OUTPUT LISTING

```
                        RE-ORDER REPORT
                        ======== ======


  ITEM      ITEM        ORDER      SUPPLIER          SUPPLIER
  CODE      DESCRIPTION QUANTITY   NAME              ADDRESS
  ----      ----------- --------   --------          --------


  A11236    BATH CABINET 750       GRIMSHAWS         12 PARK LANE
                                                     LONDON W1


  A11238    TABLE LAMP  100        VOLTAMP LTD       38 GREEN STR
                                                     BIRMINGHAM 5


  C45010    SHOWER SPRAY 150       CASSELL LTD       100 LEWES RD
                                                     PORTSMOUTH


  C56110    HEATED RAIL 100        PARKERS           CROWN HOUSE
                                                     MORDEN



*****************************************************************

     CURRENT STOCK SALES VALUE =            16328.30
     NUMBER OF DIFFERENT STOCK ITEMS ORDERED = 4


 *** RE-ORDER RUN COMPLETED ***
```

91

6 Gas Bill Preparation

GAS BILL PROGRAM SUMMARY FLOWCHART

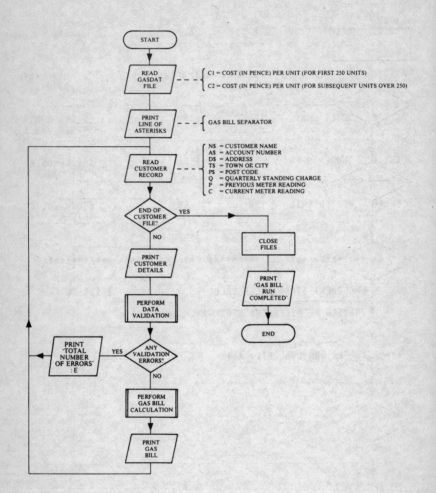

GAS BILL PROGRAM FLOWCHART –
DATA VALIDATION ROUTINE

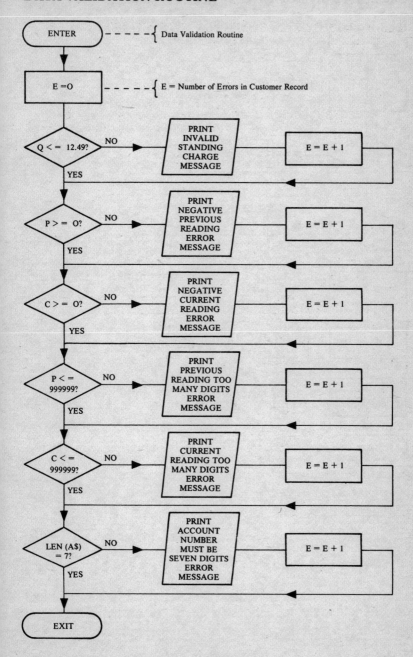

GAS BILL PROGRAM FLOWCHART – GAS BILL CALCULATION ROUTINE

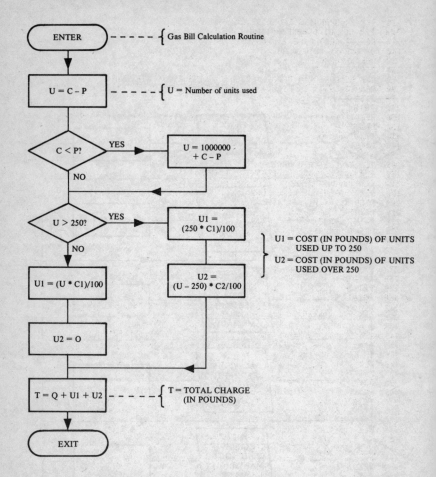

ENTER ----- { Gas Bill Calculation Routine

$U = C - P$ ----- { U = Number of units used

$C < P$? — YES → $U = 1000000 + C - P$

NO

$U > 250$? — YES → $U1 = (250 * C1)/100$

NO

$U1 = (U * C1)/100$

$U2 = (U - 250) * C2/100$

$U2 = O$

} U1 = COST (IN POUNDS) OF UNITS USED UP TO 250
U2 = COST (IN POUNDS) OF UNITS USED OVER 250

$T = Q + U1 + U2$ ----- { T = TOTAL CHARGE (IN POUNDS)

EXIT

94

GAS BILL PROGRAM LISTING

```
10   REM PROGRAMMING EXERCISE NO. 6
20   REM GAS BILL PREPARATION
30   DEFINE READ FILE #1='GASCST'
40   ON END #1 GOTO 1290
50   DEFINE READ FILE #2='GASDAT'
60   READ #2,C1,C2
70   REM C1=COST (IN PENCE) PER UNIT (FOR FIRST 250 UNITS)
80   REM C2=COST (IN PENCE) PER UNIT (FOR SUBSEQUENT UNITS OVER 250)
90   PRINT
100  PRINT
110  PRINT '*******************************************************************'
120  PRINT
130  PRINT
140  PRINT
150  REM                   READ  CUSTOMER  RECORD
160  REM N$=CUSTOMER NAME         A$=CUSTOMER ACCOUNT NUMBER
170  REM D$=CUSTOMER ADDRESS      T$=CUSTOMER TOWN
180  REM P$=POST CODE             Q = QUARTERLY STANDING CHARGE
190  REM P=PREVIOUS METER READING    C=CURRENT METER READING
200  READ #1,N$,A$,D$,T$,P$,Q,P,C
210  PRINT
220  PRINT 'NAME:        ':N$
230  PRINT 'ADDRESS:     ':D$
240  PRINT '             ':T$
250  PRINT '             ':P$
260  PRINT
270  PRINT 'ACCOUNT NO. :':A$
280  PRINT
290  PRINT
300  PRINT
310  REM           ***** DATA VALIDATION CHECKS PERFORMED *****
320  REM E = NUMBER OF ERRORS IN CUSTOMER RECORD
330  E=0
340  REM STANDING CHARGE MUST NOT BE GREATER THEN 12.49
350  R$='              (################# ######## (#'
360  IF Q<=12.49 THEN 450
370  REM INVALID STANDING CHARGE ERROR MESSAGE
380  PRINT '                    **INVALID DATA**'
390  PRINT '         **QUARTERLY STANDING CHARGE...':Q:'**'
400  PRINT '    **STANDING CHARGE MUST NOT BE GREATER THAN 12.49**'
410  PRINT
420  E=E+1
430  REM PREVIOUS READING P AND CURRENT READING C
440  REM MUST NOT BE NEGATIVE
450  IF P>=0 THEN 520
460  REM INVALID PREVIOUS READING ERROR MESSAGE
470  PRINT '                    **INVALID DATA**'
480  PRINT '           **PREVIOUS READING...':P:'**'
490  PRINT '      ***READINGS MUST BE POSITIVE NUMBERS***'
500  PRINT
510  E=E+1
520  IF C>=0 THEN 610
530  REM INVALID CURRENT READING ERROR MESSAGE
540  PRINT '            **INVALID DATA**'
550  PRINT '           **CURRENT READING...':C:'**'
560  PRINT '      ***READINGS MUST BE POSITIVE NUMBERS***'
570  PRINT
580  E=E+1
590  REM PREVIOUS READING P AND CURRENT READING C
600  REM MUST NOT BE GREATER THEN SIX DIGITS
610  IF P<=999999 THEN 670
620  PRINT '                    **INVALID DATA**'
630  PRINT USING R$,'**PREVIOUS READING...',P,'**'
640  PRINT '     **READINGS MUST BE SIX DIGIT NUMBERS**'
650  PRINT
660  E=E+1
```

95

GAS BILL PROGRAM LISTING (continued)

```
670   IF C<=999999 THEN 740
680   PRINT '                        **INVALID DATA**'
690   PRINT USING R$,'CURRENT READING....',C,'**'
700   PRINT '        **READINGS MUST BE SIX DIGIT NUMBERS**'
710   PRINT
720   E=E+1
730   REM ACCOUNT NUMBER MUST NOT BE GREATER THAN SEVEN DIGITS
740   IF LEN(A$)=7 THEN 800
750   REM INVALID ACCOUNT NUMBER ERROR MESSAGE
760   PRINT '                        **INVALID DATA**'
770   PRINT '            **ACCOUNT NUMBER MUST BE SEVEN DIGITS LONG**'
780   PRINT
790   E=E+1
800   IF E<1 THEN 870
810   PRINT
820   PRINT ' TOTAL NUMBER OF DATA ERRORS ':E
830   PRINT '********************************************************'
840   GOTO 200
850   REM          *****  MAIN  CALCULATION  PERFORMED  *****
860   REM U=TOTAL NUMBER OF UNITS USED
870   U=C-P
880   REM TEST FOR CURRENT METER READING LESS THAN PREVIOUS
890   IF C<P THEN  U=1.E+06+C-P
900   REM
910   REM U1=COST OF UNITS USED UPTO 250
920   REM U2=COST OF UNITS USED OVER 250
930   IF U>250 THEN 970
940   U1=(U*C1)/100
950   U2=0
960   GOTO 990
970   U1=(250*C1)/100
980   U2=(U-250)*C2/100
990   REM CALCULATE TOTAL CHARGE T (IN POUNDS)
1000  T=Q+U1+U2
1010  REM
1020  REM         *****  GAS BILL PRINTING IS PERFORMED  *****
1030  M$='(#########      (########       (####'
1040  Q$='  ######         ######          ######'
1050  PRINT USING M$,'PREVIOUS',' CURRENT','UNITS'
1060  PRINT USING M$,' READING',' READING',' USED'
1070  PRINT USING M$,'********',' *******','*****'
1080  PRINT USING Q$,P,C,U
1090  PRINT
1100  PRINT
1110  X$='       (################## #.## (################## ##.##'
1120  PRINT USING X$,'**FIRST 250 UNITS @',C1,'P PER UNIT... ... ...',U1
1130  IF U2=0 THEN 1160
1140  Y$='       (################## #### (## #.## (########### ##.##'
1150  PRINT USING Y$,'**SUBSEQUENT UNITS(',(U-250),') @',C2,'P PER UNIT..',U2
1160  Z$='       (##################         #### (## #.##'
1170  PRINT USING Z$,'**QUARTERLY STANDING CHARGE... ... ... ...',Q
1180  PRINT '                                          ======='
1190  K$='       (##################         ####.##'
1200  PRINT USING K$,'TOTAL CHARGE (IN POUNDS)',T
1210  PRINT '                                          ======='
1220  PRINT
1230  PRINT
1240  PRINT '********************************************************'
1250  PRINT
1260  PRINT
1270  PRINT
1280  GOTO 200
1290  CLOSE #1
1300  CLOSE #2
1310  PRINT
1320  PRINT '     ***GAS BILL RUN COMPLETED***'
1330  END
```

GAS BILL DATA FILE – GASCST

```
J AVERY                    S R PATEL
1001116                    1001140
124 WHITTON DENE           72 SPELDHURST ROAD
LONDON                     LONDON
W6 5PT                     W4 4TT
6.12                       12.49
450012                     540023
451410                     540267
K S BHULLAR                D P REBBECK
1001124                    1001159
58 LEIGHTON GDNS           92 HANOVER ROAD
LONDON                     LONDON
NW10                       NW10
12.49                      12.50
811203                     -000450
812649                     001346
R A FRANCIS                J A TREVETT
1001132                    1001167
83 HAIG ROAD               4 APPLEYARD COURT
LONDON                     LONDON
W5 5RF                     W5 4RL
12.49                      6.12
998882                     2211765
000950                     2213346
```

GAS BILL DATA FILE – GASDAT

```
5.50, 3.65
```

97

GAS BILL OUTPUT LISTING

```
*****************************************************************

NAME:        J AVERY
ADDRESS:     124 WHITTON DENE
             LONDON
             W6 5PT

ACCOUNT NO.: 1001116


PREVIOUS                   CURRENT                     UNITS
 READING                   READING                     USED
********                   *******                     *****
  450012                    451410                     1398


     **FIRST 250 UNITS @ 5.50 P PER UNIT... ... ... 13.75
     **SUBSEQUENT UNITS< 1148 > @ 3.65 P PER UNIT.. 41.90
     **QUARTERLY STANDING CHARGE... ... ... ... ...  6.12
                                                    =======
                    TOTAL CHARGE (IN POUNDS)        61.77
                                                    =======


*****************************************************************

NAME:        K S BHULLAR
ADDRESS:     58 LEIGHTON GDNS
             LONDON
             NW10

ACCOUNT NO.: 1001124


PREVIOUS                   CURRENT                     UNITS
 READING                   READING                     USED
********                   *******                     *****
  811203                    812649                     1446


     **FIRST 250 UNITS @ 5.50 P PER UNIT... ... ... 13.75
     **SUBSEQUENT UNITS< 1196 > @ 3.65 P PER UNIT.. 43.65
     **QUARTERLY STANDING CHARGE... ... ... ... ... 12.49
                                                    =======
                    TOTAL CHARGE (IN POUNDS)        69.89
                                                    =======
```

98

GAS BILL OUTPUT LISTING (continued)

```
**********************************************************************


NAME:        R A FRANCIS
ADDRESS:     83 HAIG ROAD
             LONDON
             W5 5RF

ACCOUNT NO.: 1001132


PREVIOUS                  CURRENT                    UNITS
READING                   READING                    USED
********                  *******                    *****
  998882                    950                      2068


     **FIRST 250 UNITS @ 5.50 P PER UNIT.. .. .. ... 13.75
     **SUBSEQUENT UNITS( 1818 ) @ 3.65 P PER UNIT.. 66.36
     **QUARTERLY STANDING CHARGE... ... ... ... ... 12.49
                                                    =======
                    TOTAL CHARGE (IN POUNDS)         92.60
                                                    =======


**********************************************************************


NAME:        S R PATEL
ADDRESS:     72 SPELDHURST ROAD
             LONDON
             W4 4TT

ACCOUNT NO.: 1001140


PREVIOUS                  CURRENT                    UNITS
READING                   READING                    USED
********                  *******                    *****
  540023                    540267                    244


     **FIRST 250 UNITS @ 5.50 P PER UNIT... ... ... 13.42
     **QUARTERLY STANDING CHARGE... ... ... ... ... 12.49
                                                    =======
                    TOTAL CHARGE (IN POUNDS)         25.91
                                                    =======
```

99

GAS BILL OUTPUT LISTING (continued)

```
**********************************************************************
```

```
NAME:        D P REBBECK
ADDRESS:     92 HANOVER ROAD
             LONDON
             NW10

ACCOUNT NO.: 1001159


                    **INVALID DATA**
          **QUARTERLY STANDING CHARGE... 12.5 **
     **STANDING CHARGE MUST NOT BE GREATER THAN 12.49**

                    **INVALID DATA**
             **PREVIOUS READING... -450 **
          ***READINGS MUST BE POSITIVE NUMBERS***


 TOTAL NUMBER OF DATA ERRORS  2
**********************************************************************
NAME:        J A TREVETT
ADDRESS:     4 APPLEYARD COURT
             LONDON
             W5 4RL

ACCOUNT NO.: 1001167


                    **INVALID DATA**
             **PREVIOUS READING...  2211760 **
          **READINGS MUST BE SIX DIGIT NUMBERS**

                    **INVALID DATA**
             CURRENT READING....   2213340 **
          **READINGS MUST BE SIX DIGIT NUMBERS**


 TOTAL NUMBER OF DATA ERRORS  2
**********************************************************************

      ***GAS BILL RUN COMPLETED***
```

7 Credit Card Statement Preparation

CREDIT CARD STATEMENT DATA FILE – CARDAT

```
J AMERY
94.27
94.27
8,DEC,80
7,NOV,80
ALLDERS OF SUTTON
15.50
10,NOV,80
WRIGHTS GARAGE CROYDON
11.25
99,XXX,99
V GONZALES
42.50
34.25
8,DEC,80
12,NOV,80
BENTALLS OF EALING
75.20
12,NOV,80
BENTALLS OF EALING
40.00
18,NOV,80
SUPERDRUG BRENTFORD
6.45
29,NOV,80
BARTHOLOMEW & SONS ACTON
14.32
99,XXX,99
P PARTRIDGE
155.43
95.43
8,DEC,80
11,NOV,80
HARRODS KNIGHTSBRIDGE
240.00
99,XXX,99
```

```
PD MANN
60.00
10.00
8,DEC,80
27,NOV,80
POOH CORNER BATTERSEA
57.60
28,NOV,80
GREAT AMERICAN DISASTER CHELSEA
15.42
28,NOV,80
BOOTS FULHAM
5.30
99,XXX,99
LAST,4,10,352.35,481.04
```

CREDIT CARD STATEMENT OUTPUT LISTING

```
============================================================

                  CREDIT CARD STATEMENT
                  ----------------------


        P PARTRIDGE                        8 DEC 80


    DATE            DETAILS                AMOUNT
    ----            -------                ------



                BALANCE FROM PREVIOUS STATEMENT   155.43
                PAYMENT RECEIVED-THANK YOU          95.43 CR
                INTEREST AT 2.5 PER CENT PER MONTH   1.50
                                                  ----------
                BALANCE BROUGHT FORWARD             61.50
    11 NOV 80   HARRODS KNIGHTSBRIDGE              240.00




                                          ----------
                        PRESENT BALANCE   301.50


============================================================

                  CREDIT CARD STATEMENT
                  ----------------------


        PD MANN                            8 DEC 80


    DATE            DETAILS                AMOUNT
    ----            -------                ------



                BALANCE FROM PREVIOUS STATEMENT    60.00
                PAYMENT RECEIVED-THANK YOU          10.00 CR
                INTEREST AT 2.5 PER CENT PER MONTH   1.25
                                                  ----------
                BALANCE BROUGHT FORWARD             51.25
    27 NOV 80   POOH CORNER BATTERSEA               57.60
    28 NOV 80   GREAT AMERICAN DISASTER CHELSEA     15.42
    28 NOV 80   BOOTS FULHAM                         5.30




                                          ----------
                        PRESENT BALANCE   129.57
```

103

CREDIT CARD STATEMENT OUTPUT LISTING (continued)

```
===========================================================
                    CREDIT CARD STATEMENT
                    ----------------------


        J AMERY                              8 DEC 80


    DATE              DETAILS                  AMOUNT
    ----              -------                  ------


                  BALANCE FROM PREVIOUS STATEMENT   94.27
                  PAYMENT RECEIVED-THANK YOU        94.27 CR
                                              ----------
                  BALANCE BROUGHT FORWARD           0.00
  7 NOV 80        ALLDERS OF SUTTON                15.50
 10 NOV 80        WRIGHTS GARAGE CROYDON           11.25




                                              ----------
                       PRESENT BALANCE        26.75


===========================================================
                    CREDIT CARD STATEMENT
                    ----------------------

        V GONZALES                           8 DEC 80


    DATE              DETAILS                  AMOUNT
    ----              -------                  ------


                  BALANCE FROM PREVIOUS STATEMENT   42.50
                  PAYMENT RECEIVED-THANK YOU        34.25 CR
                  INTEREST AT 2.5 PER CENT PER MONTH  0.21
                                              ----------
                  BALANCE BROUGHT FORWARD           8.46
 12 NOV 80        BENTALLS OF EALING               75.20
 12 NOV 80        BENTALLS OF EALING               40.00
 18 NOV 80        SUPERDRUG BRENTFORD               6.45
 29 NOV 80        BARTHOLOMEW & SONS ACTON         14.32




                                              ----------
                       PRESENT BALANCE       144.43
```

104

CREDIT CARD STATEMENT OUTPUT LISTING
(CONTROL REPORT)

```
***********************************************************

                    CONTROL STATEMENT
                    -----------------


DETAILS                              FILE   ACTUAL ERROR
-------                              ----   ------ -----
NO OF CUSTOMERS ON FILE              4.00    4.00
NO OF TRANSACTIONS ON FILE          10.00   10.00
TOTAL OF PREVIOUS OUTSTANDING BALS  352.35 352.20    0.15
TOTAL OF TRANSACTIONS ON FILE       481.04 481.04


===========================================================

RUN COMPLETED
```

105

8 Company Sales Report

COMPANY SALES REPORT OUTPUT LISTING

YEAR 1 DATA ANALYSIS

THE HIGHEST SALE OF 224 THOUSAND BTLS. IS IN APRIL
THE LOWEST SALE OF 119 THOUSAND BTLS. IS IN NOVEMBER
THE MEAN SALES OF THE YEAR IS 175.75 THOUSAND BTLS
THE STD. DEVIATION OF THE SALES IS 42.1982 THOUSAND BTLS
SALES FIGURES OF THE YEAR AS A HISTOGRAM

```
MONTH             NO OF BOTTLES (SALES)
                  0    50   100   150   200   250   300   350
-----------I----I----I----I----I----I----I----I-
JANUARY    I XXXXXXXXXXXXXXXXXXX ( 199 )
FEBRUARY   I XXXXXXXXXXXXXXXXXXXXX ( 211 )
MARCH      I XXXXXXXXXXXXXXXXXXXXX ( 210 )
APRIL      I XXXXXXXXXXXXXXXXXXXXXX ( 224 )
MAY        I XXXXXXXXXXXXXXXXXXXXXX ( 220 )
JUNE       I XXXXXXXXXXXXXXXXXXXXX ( 210 )
JULY       I XXXXXXXXXXXXXXXXXXXX ( 200 )
AUGUST     I XXXXXXXXXXXXXX ( 145 )
SEPTEMBER  I XXXXXXXXXXXXX ( 130 )
OCTOBER    I XXXXXXXXXXXX ( 121 )
NOVEMBER   I XXXXXXXXXXX ( 119 )
DECEMBER   I XXXXXXXXXXXX ( 120 )
```

YEAR 2 DATA ANALYSIS

THE HIGHEST SALE OF 301 THOUSAND BTLS. IS IN JUNE
THE LOWEST SALE OF 160 THOUSAND BTLS. IS IN SEPTEMBER
THE MEAN SALES OF THE YEAR IS 242.667 THOUSAND BTLS
THE STD. DEVIATION OF THE SALES IS 60.2167 THOUSAND BTLS
SALES FIGURES OF THE YEAR AS A HISTOGRAM

```
MONTH             NO OF BOTTLES (SALES)
                  0    50   100   150   200   250   300   350
-----------I----I----I----I----I----I----I----I-
JANUARY    I XXXXXXXXXXXXXXXXXXXXXXXXXXXXX ( 287 )
FEBRUARY   I XXXXXXXXXXXXXXXXXXXXXXXXXXXXXX ( 291 )
MARCH      I XXXXXXXXXXXXXXXXXXXXXXXXXXXXXX ( 294 )
APRIL      I XXXXXXXXXXXXXXXXXXXXXXXXXXXXXX ( 299 )
MAY        I XXXXXXXXXXXXXXXXXXXXXXXXXXXXXX ( 299 )
JUNE       I XXXXXXXXXXXXXXXXXXXXXXXXXXXXXXX ( 301 )
JULY       I XXXXXXXXXXXXXXXXXXXXXXXXXXXXX ( 280 )
AUGUST     I XXXXXXXXXXXXXXXXXXX ( 190 )
SEPTEMBER  I XXXXXXXXXXXXXXXX ( 160 )
OCTOBER    I XXXXXXXXXXXXXXXXX ( 171 )
NOVEMBER   I XXXXXXXXXXXXXXXX ( 162 )
DECEMBER   I XXXXXXXXXXXXXXXXX ( 178 )
```

106

COMPANY SALES REPORT OUTPUT LISTING (continued)

YEAR 3 DATA ANALYSIS

THE HIGHEST SALE OF 348 THOUSAND BTLS. IS IN MAY
THE LOWEST SALE OF 180 THOUSAND BTLS. IS IN OCTOBER
THE MEAN SALES OF THE YEAR IS 273.167 THOUSAND BTLS
THE STD. DEVIATION OF THE SALES IS 58.212 THOUSAND BTLS
SALES FIGURES OF THE YEAR AS A HISTOGRAM

```
MONTH            NO OF BOTTLES (SALES)
                 0    50   100   150   200   250   300   350
----------I----I----I----I----I----I----I----I-
JANUARY    I XXXXXXXXXXXXXXXXXXXXXXXXXXXXXX ( 300 )
FEBRUARY   I XXXXXXXXXXXXXXXXXXXXXXXXXXXXXXX ( 310 )
MARCH      I XXXXXXXXXXXXXXXXXXXXXXXXXXXXXX ( 305 )
APRIL      I XXXXXXXXXXXXXXXXXXXXXXXXXXXXXXXXXX ( 340 )
MAY        I XXXXXXXXXXXXXXXXXXXXXXXXXXXXXXXXXX ( 348 )
JUNE       I XXXXXXXXXXXXXXXXXXXXXXXXXXXXXXXXX ( 335 )
JULY       I XXXXXXXXXXXXXXXXXXXXXXXXXXXXXX ( 295 )
AUGUST     I XXXXXXXXXXXXXXXXXXXXXXXXX ( 250 )
SEPTEMBER  I XXXXXXXXXXXXXXXXXXXXX ( 210 )
OCTOBER    I XXXXXXXXXXXXXXXXXX ( 180 )
NOVEMBER   I XXXXXXXXXXXXXXXXXXXX ( 200 )
DECEMBER   I XXXXXXXXXXXXXXXXXXXX ( 205 )
```

```
                      **********
                      **********
```

```
**************************************************************
SALES YEAR                    YEAR 1   YEAR 2   YEAR 3
**************************************************************
TOTAL SALES (1000 STAND BOTS.)  2109     2912     3278

PEAK MONTHLY SALES FIGURE        224      301      348

LOWEST MONTHLY SALES FIGURE      119      160      180

MEAN MONTHLY SALE             175.75   242.667  273.167

TOTAL SALES INDEX (YR 1 BASE)    100   138.075  155.429
**************************************************************
```

107

10 Student Marks

STUDENT MARKS PROGRAM LISTING

```
10    REM PROGRAMMING EXERCISE NO. 10
20    W$='               <##########################    ###.# %'
30    Z$='              <#######    <#######    <#########    <#########'
40    Y$=' <#########       ###         ###         ###         ###'
50    X$=' <####          <#          <#          <#          <#'
60    L$='            <######                  <############'
70    M$='            <#########           ###.#'
80    DEFINE READ FILE #1='MARKS'
90    ON END #1 GOTO 780
100   PRINT TAB(25):'STUDENT PASS LIST REPORT'
110   PRINT TAB(25):'========================'
120   PRINT
130   PRINT
140   READ #1,N
150   READ #1,N$
160   READ #1,A1,E1,S1,C1
170   READ #1,A2,E2,S2,C2
180   REM C IS COUNT OF NUMBER OF RECORDS
190   C=C+1
200   S=A1+A2+E1+E2+S1+S2+C1+C2
210   REM RUNNING TOTALS OF MARKS IN EACH SUBJECT STORED IN A3, E3, S3 AND C3
220   A3=A3+A1+A2
230   E3=E3+E1+E2
240   S3=S3+S1+S2
250   C3=C3+C1+C2
260   X1=A1
270   X2=A2
280   GOSUB 640
290   REM RUNNING PASS TOTALS IN EACH SUBJECT STORED IN A4, E4, S4 AND C4
300   IF G$<>'F' THEN   A4=A4+1
310   A$=G$
320   X1=E1
330   X2=E2
340   GOSUB 640
350   IF G$<>'F' THEN   E4=E4+1
360   E$=G$
370   X1=S1
380   X2=S2
390   GOSUB 640
400   IF G$<>'F' THEN   S4=S4+1
410   S$=G$
420   X1=C1
430   X2=C2
440   GOSUB 640
450   IF G$<>'F' THEN   C4=C4+1
460   C$=G$
470   PRINT
480   PRINT
490   PRINT '   STUDENT NAME:':TAB(18):N$:TAB(45):'STUDENT NO:':TAB(58):N
500   PRINT USING Z$,'ACCOUNTS','ECONOMICS','STATISTICS','COMPUTING'
510   PRINT USING Y$,'EXAM',A1,E1,S1,C1
520   PRINT USING Y$,'COURSEWORK',A2,E2,S2,C2
530   PRINT USING X$,'GRADE',A$,E$,S$,C$
540   PRINT
550   PRINT
560   IF S>350 THEN   Y$='PROCEED'
570   IF S<=350 THEN   Y$='REPEAT'
580   PRINT TAB(35):'OVERALL RESULT = ':Y$
590   PRINT
600   PRINT
610   GOTO 140
```

108

STUDENT MARKS PROGRAM LISTING (continued)

```
620   REM GRADE ASSIGNMENT SUBROUTINE
630   REM AFTER SUBROUTINE EXECUTION SUBJECT GRADE IS STORED IN G$
640   IF X1<70 THEN   GOTO 680
650   IF X2<70 THEN   GOTO 680
660   G$='D'
670   RETURN
680   IF X1<55 THEN   GOTO 720
690   IF X2<55 THEN   GOTO 720
700   G$='C'
710   RETURN
720   IF X1<40 THEN   GOTO 760
730   IF X2<40 THEN   GOTO 760
740   G$='P'
750   RETURN
760   G$='F'
770   RETURN
780   PRINT
790   PRINT
800   PRINT TAB(25):'SUMMARY REPORT'
810   PRINT TAB(25):'=============='
820   PRINT
830   PRINT
840   REM SUMMARY REPORT PRINTING
850   REM PERCENTAGE PASS RATE REPORT
860   PRINT USING L$,'SUBJECT','%GE PASS RATE'
870   PRINT USING L$,'-------','-------------'
880   PRINT USING M$,'ACCOUNTS',A4/C*100
890   PRINT USING M$,'ECONOMICS',E4/C*100
900   PRINT USING M$,'STATISTICS',S4/C*100
910   PRINT USING M$,'COMPUTING',C4/C*100
920   C=C*2
930   PRINT
940   PRINT
950   PRINT
960   REM AVERAGE MARK REPORT
970   PRINT USING W$,'AVERAGE ACCOUNTS MARK IS ',A3/C
980   PRINT USING W$,'AVERAGE ECONOMICS MARK IS ',E3/C
990   PRINT USING W$,'AVERAGE STATISTICS MARK IS ',S3/C
1000  PRINT USING W$,'AVERAGE COMPUTING MARK IS ',C3/C
1010  PRINT
1020  PRINT TAB(25):'RUN COMPLETED'
1030  END
```

109

STUDENT MARKS DATA FILE – MARKS

```
2056
P ADAMS
58,75,40,66
60,71,55,80
2057
J M ANDOPOLOUS
45,52,35,36
50,54,42,37
2058
F M GREAVES
56,65,42,62
62,65,61,70
2059
J GHATRI
35,42,42,15
20,36,30,28
2060
L M PEEVERS
53,52,30,40
53,54,28,40
2061
G PAYTON
42,45,41,39
50,52,46,42
2062
M ROBERTS
48,62,45,43
58,69,65,68
2063
F ROYSTON
72,76,56,71
75,65,69,85
```

STUDENT MARKS OUTPUT LISTING

```
                    STUDENT PASS LIST REPORT
                    ========================


STUDENT NAME:  P ADAMS                  STUDENT NO:  2056
               ACCOUNTS    ECONOMICS   STATISTICS   COMPUTING
EXAM             58           75           40          66
COURSEWORK       60           71           55          80
GRADE            C            D            P           C


                              OVERALL RESULT =  PROCEED




STUDENT NAME:  J M ANDOPOLOUS           STUDENT NO:  2057
               ACCOUNTS    ECONOMICS   STATISTICS   COMPUTING
EXAM             45           52           35          36
COURSEWORK       50           54           42          37
GRADE            P            P            F           F


                              OVERALL RESULT =  PROCEED




STUDENT NAME:  F M GREAVES              STUDENT NO:  2058
               ACCOUNTS    ECONOMICS   STATISTICS   COMPUTING
EXAM             56           65           42          62
COURSEWORK       62           65           61          70
GRADE            C            C            P           C


                              OVERALL RESULT =  PROCEED




STUDENT NAME:  J GHATRI                 STUDENT NO:  2059
               ACCOUNTS    ECONOMICS   STATISTICS   COMPUTING
EXAM             35           42           42          15
COURSEWORK       20           36           30          28
GRADE            F            F            F           F


                              OVERALL RESULT =  REPEAT




STUDENT NAME:  L M PEEVERS              STUDENT NO:  2060
               ACCOUNTS    ECONOMICS   STATISTICS   COMPUTING
EXAM             53           52           30          40
COURSEWORK       53           54           28          40
GRADE            P            P            F           P


                              OVERALL RESULT =  REPEAT
```

111

STUDENT MARKS OUTPUT LISTING (continued)

```
STUDENT NAME:  G PAYTON                      STUDENT NO:  2061
               ACCOUNTS     ECONOMICS    STATISTICS    COMPUTING
EXAM              42           45           41           39
COURSEWORK        50           52           46           42
GRADE             P            P            P            F


                           OVERALL RESULT =  PROCEED



STUDENT NAME:  M ROBERTS                     STUDENT NO:  2062
               ACCOUNTS     ECONOMICS    STATISTICS    COMPUTING
EXAM              48           62           45           43
COURSEWORK        58           69           65           68
GRADE             P            C            P            P


                           OVERALL RESULT =  PROCEED



STUDENT NAME:  F ROYSTON                     STUDENT NO:  2063
               ACCOUNTS     ECONOMICS    STATISTICS    COMPUTING
EXAM              72           76           56           71
COURSEWORK        75           65           69           85
GRADE             D            C            C            D


                           OVERALL RESULT =  PROCEED



                           SUMMARY REPORT
                           ==============



           SUBJECT                 %GE PASS RATE
           -------                 -------------
           ACCOUNTS                    87.5
           ECONOMICS                   87.5
           STATISTICS                  62.5
           COMPUTING                   62.5



           AVERAGE ACCOUNTS MARK IS      52.3 %
           AVERAGE ECONOMICS MARK IS     58.4 %
           AVERAGE STATISTICS MARK IS    45.4 %
           AVERAGE COMPUTING MARK IS     51.4 %

                    RUN COMPLETED
```

112

Appendix A System Flowchart Symbols

SYMBOLS FOR MEDIA HOLDING DATA

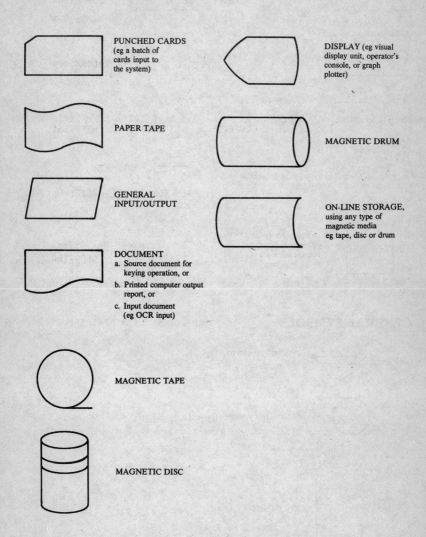

PUNCHED CARDS
(eg a batch of
cards input to
the system)

DISPLAY (eg visual
display unit, operator's
console, or graph
plotter)

PAPER TAPE

MAGNETIC DRUM

GENERAL
INPUT/OUTPUT

ON-LINE STORAGE,
using any type of
magnetic media
eg tape, disc or drum

DOCUMENT
a. Source document for
   keying operation, or
b. Printed computer output
   report, or
c. Input document
   (eg OCR input)

MAGNETIC TAPE

MAGNETIC DISC

113

SYMBOLS FOR OPERATIONS:

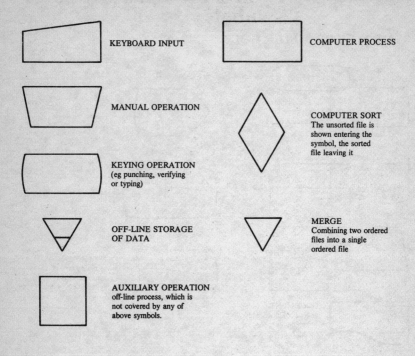

KEYBOARD INPUT

COMPUTER PROCESS

MANUAL OPERATION

COMPUTER SORT
The unsorted file is
shown entering the
symbol, the sorted
file leaving it

KEYING OPERATION
(eg punching, verifying
or typing)

OFF-LINE STORAGE
OF DATA

MERGE
Combining two ordered
files into a single
ordered file

AUXILIARY OPERATION
off-line process, which is
not covered by any of
above symbols.

GENERAL SYMBOLS

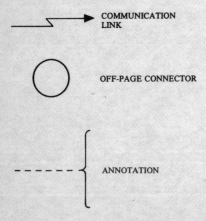

COMMUNICATION
LINK

OFF-PAGE CONNECTOR

ANNOTATION

*NOTE: The British Standards Institution and the leading computer manu-
facturers publish their own similar sets of symbols.*

Appendix B Program Flowchart Symbols

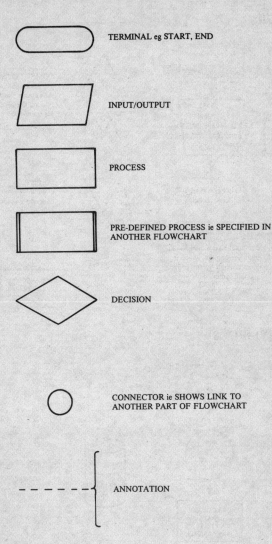

TERMINAL eg START, END

INPUT/OUTPUT

PROCESS

PRE-DEFINED PROCESS ie SPECIFIED IN
ANOTHER FLOWCHART

DECISION

CONNECTOR ie SHOWS LINK TO
ANOTHER PART OF FLOWCHART

ANNOTATION

Appendix C System Flowchart of Simplified Weekly Payroll

MAIN PROCESSING ROUTINE

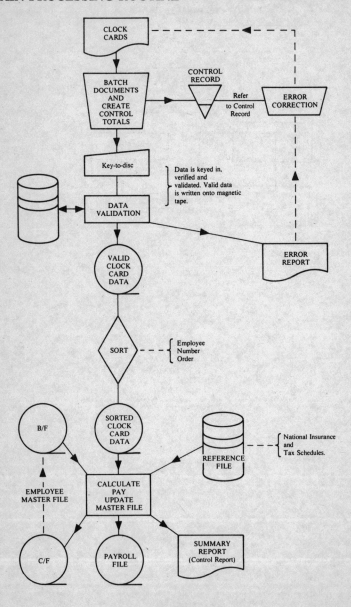

PAYROLL PRINTING ROUTINE

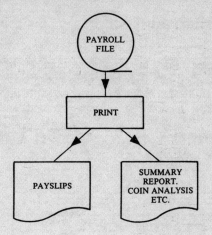

Appendix D Summary of BASIC Statements

The BASIC statements that are used in the examples in the programming exercises are classified into SIX categories and are simply listed in this Appendix. The final section of this Appendix indicates the major differences between the PRIME version (which is the one used) and other versions.

Arithmetic Operators

+	ADD
–	SUBTRACT
*	MULTIPLY
/	DIVIDE
↑ **** }	RAISE TO POWER

Relational Operators

=	EQUALS
<	LESS THAN
<= =< }	LESS THAN OR EQUAL TO
>	GREATER THAN
>= => }	GREATER THAN OR EQUAL TO
<>	NOT EQUAL TO

INPUT/OUTPUT STATEMENTS

```
READ      X, Y, Z, N$
DATA      14.5, 680, 32, 'JAMES'
INPUT     A, B, C
DEFINE    READ FILE #1 = 'CUSTOMER'
DEFINE    FILE #2 = 'NEWFILE'
READ      #1, N$, C1, C2
WRITE     #2, C$, T1, T2, T3
PRINT     'SUM OF NUMBERS IS', S
PRINTUSING A$, X, Y, Z
ON END #1 GOTO 200
CLOSE #1
```

118

Assignment Statements

LET $S = 0$ (or $S = 0$)

$R1 = (-B + SQR\ (B*B - 4*A*C))/(2*A)$

$R2 = (-B - SQR\ (B*B - 4*A*C))/(2*A)$

N$ = 'JAMES'

Control Statements

GOTO 100

GOSUB 500

RETURN

IF A<B THEN GOTO 100

IF X$ = 'YES' THEN PRINT 'ACCEPT'

IF X = 1 THEN C = C + 1

FOR J = 1 TO 100 STEP 1

FOR J = 1, 10, 1

FOR J = 100, 1, -1

NEXT J

ON (J - 2) GOTO 10, 50, 100

STOP

CONTINUE

END

Standard Functions

SIN (X)	SINE OF X, WHERE X IS IN RADIANS
COS (X)	COSINE OF X, WHERE X IS IN RADIANS
TAN (X)	TANGENT OF X, WHERE X IS IN RADIANS
ATN (X)	ARCTANGENT OF X IN RADIANS ie THE ANGLE WHOSE TANGENT IS X
LOG (X)	NATURAL LOGARITHM OF X, WHERE X IS GREATER THAN ZERO
EXP (X)	EXPONENTIAL OF X ie CONSTANT 'E' IS RAISED TO POWER OF X
SQR (X)	SQUARE ROOT OF X, WHERE X IS GREATER THAN ZERO
ABS (X)	ABSOLUTE VALUE OF X
SGN (X)	SIGN OF X (ie -1 IF X<0, 0 if X = 0, +1 IF X>0)
INT (X)	INTEGER VALUE OF X (ie LARGEST INTEGER LESS THAN OR EQUAL TO THE VARIABLE)
RND (X)	GENERATES A RANDOM NUMBER BETWEEN 0 and 1
LEN (X$)	CALCULATES THE LENGTH OF THE STRING HELD IN X$

N.B. X MAY BE ANY VALID EXPRESSION

Major differences between PRIME version of BASIC and other versions (for purposes of undertaking the given programming exercises)

1. The PRINTUSING statement is designed to give precise layout on output. It works by building up an image of the required position of each output field and using this image at the time of printing. The image for each field is defined using the hash symbol #, which represents a single character.

Example 1. Printing of Name and Nett Pay

X$ = '   <###########   ###.##   '

PRINTUSING   X$, N$, P

Notes: The < sign indicates that the value of the name is to be left justified on output.

Sufficient hash symbols must be included for a given field. If there are insufficient hash symbols for an alpha-numeric field, then the value will be truncated; for a numeric field the value will not be printed, instead a series of asterisks will appear to warn the user.

In the above example, the maximum number of characters in the name field is 12; and in the pay field, the maximum value is 999.99

2. The PRIME version of BASIC allows strings to be stored in variables whose name consists of a letter followed by a dollar sign eg A$, X$ are valid names, and C$ = 'TYRE CO LTD' is a valid assignment statement using a string variable.

3. The PRIME version of BASIC allows arrays, which may hold numeric values or strings. Arrays are assigned specific dimensions in a DIM statement eg a one dimensional numeric array B would be defined as DIM B(100); this allocates 100 elements which may be referred to as B(1), B(2) . . . . . B(100). (N.B. B(0) is also implicitly defined)

A string array, such as A$(100), means that there are strings by the names A$(1), A$(2) . . . . . A$(100).

In many other versions of BASIC it is not possible to do this and DIM A$(100) would specify one string variable, which contains up to 100 characters.

4. The PRIME version does not allow the placing of a number of instructions on a single line.

Aims of the Manuals

To give *comprehensive* coverage of specific examination syllabuses in a *simplified* manner and at an economic price i.e. one which most students would be willing to pay either as a main text book or as supplementary study material.

Types of Manuals

There are two types of manuals:

1. *Instructional manuals* — little, or no knowledge on the part of the student is assumed. The basic principles of the subject are presented in an easily assimilated form — manageable study areas with introductions and summaries. The *many questions* at the end of study areas *(answers at the back of the manual)* can be used for classroom confirmation of understanding or as a basis for discussion. Ideal for releasing valuable classroom time for concentration on *practice* of principles and teaching the more difficult areas. Perfect for *self study* where students have missed classes due to starting late, sickness etc. and for *revision purposes.* The tabular layout is designed to eliminate the need for note taking.

2. *Practice manuals* — knowledge of the basic principles is assumed. Using specially selected past examination questions from the *main examination areas*, fully worked solutions show the student *how to tackle* the particular question and guides him through the answer in such a way as to enable the student to pinpoint his problem areas — and thus to overcome them. Ideal for *confirmation* of understanding of each study area prior to going on to new fields, as well as *practice* before progress tests and the examination.

Management: Theory and Practice G.A. Cole

This manual aims to provide, in one concise volume, the principal ideas and developments in the theory and practice of management as required by business and accountancy students.

It is thus principally aimed at providing a course textbook for students sitting ACCA, ICMA, ICSA and IOB. It will also be useful to students taking management topics in the examination of the IOM, IIM and IAM.

Relatively few books on management are written specifically for business and accountancy students and those that are on the market do not usually develop the links between the subject matter and the examinations set by the professional bodies. This manual aims to fill that gap.

Contents

Introduction to Management Theory
  Background Developments
  Definitions and Interpretations
Classical Theories
  Henri Fayol
  F.W. Taylor and the Scientific Management School
  The Contribution of Urwick & Brech
  The Concept of Bureaucracy
Human Relations Theories
  Motivation and Assumptions about People
  The Impact of Elton Mayo
  Major Theories of Human Motivation
Systems Approaches to Management Theory
  Organisations as Systems
  Socio-technical Systems/Developments in Systems Theories
  Contingency Approaches to Management
Management in Practice: Introduction
  The Process of Management
Policy, Planning and Decision-making
  Decision-making
  Organization Objectives and Corporate Planning
  Management by Objectives
  Man-Power Planning

Organizing and Communicating
  The Process of Organizing
  Organization Structures
  Line and Staff Relationships
  Organization Development Techniques
  The Role of External Consultants
  Formal Communication in Organizations
  Committees
Leadership and Delegation
  Types of Leadership
  Management Styles
  Delegation and the Span of Control
Control in Management
  Common Methods of Control
  Techniques for Control
Functional Management: Introduction
  Specialist Functions in Management
Marketing Management
  The Marketing Concept
  Marketing Research
  Marketing and Sales Management
Production Management
  Types of Production
  Basic Elements of Production
  Organization of a Production Department
Personnel Management
  The Role of the Personnel Function
  Recruitment and Selection
  Training and Development
  Job Evaluation
  Employee Relations, Trade Unions and Collective Bargaining
  Legal Aspects of Employment

Appendices
Outline Answers to Examination Questions
Commentary and Fuller Answers to Further Examination Questions
Guide to Examination Technique
Glossary of Management Terms
Selected Examination Questions without Answers

Gerald Cole is Senior Lecturer in Management Studies, Department of Management and Organizational Studies, Luton College of Higher Education.
Note to Lecturers: Answer Supplement available (see inside front cover of catalogue).

450 pages (approx): June 1982: ISBN 0 905435 26 5

Auditing
A.H. Millichamp 2nd Edition

The manual is designed to provide a simplified but thorough approach to the understanding of modern auditing theory and practice. It is particularly suited to students preparing themselves for the examinations of ICA, ACCA and IAS (it is prescribed reading for ACCA) but is also suitable for those studying Auditing as part of a Higher National Diploma or Certificate course in business studies.

"Mr. Millichamp certainly has a commendable command of the subject matter which he is able to convey in the course of his book . . . . it was interesting to note the effect of block capital headings at each relevant stage so that the student is not confused by the task of trying to assimilate unrelated points under the same heading. The chapters lead the student both into the subject matter and, at the right stage, the details related to the subject matter. This aspect is important in answering examination questions . . . . . . the author has adopted an informal and chatty style of addressing the reader, but such informality does not detract from the precision in the layout of the information and instruction to be imparted . . . . the questions and answers and appendices should leave a student in no doubt as to the need for precise language in reports and other forms of communication . . . . . the author has quite rightly assumed that when a candidate studies the subject matter of auditing he will bring to bear such knowledge on accounting procedures and law which will have been learned in separate courses of study. The book has no frills; it is packed with essential and relevant information set out in an easily assimilated manner and is designed to assist a student in presenting a good paper at his examination"
Review extract Certified Accountants Students Newsletter

"An excellent book", "Well presented and gives great assistance through the course and during revision"
Lecturers comments

"Without doubt the best text for examination preparation I have read"
Students comment

Contents

The author is Senior lecturer in Accounting at the Polytechnic, Wolverhampton.

Note to Lecturers: Answer Supplement available (see inside front cover of catalogue).

480 pages: 1981: ISBN 0 905435 21 4

Financial Accounting

A.R. Jennings

Manual 1

Manual 2

These manuals are, together, aimed at providing in an instructional manner, the information needed by students to approach with confidence the professional level examinations of the ACCA and ICMA. There is also substantial coverage of the ICA examination requirements and the financial accounting content of relevant degree courses.

A vast number of books have been written on Financial Accounting but they tend to teach principles only without relating those principles to the specific requirements of professional level examinations.

These manuals *instruct* the student to be able to answer the questions that are *actually set* at professional level.

"This book is a credit to its author and publisher; without doubt it achieves its objective of providing the student with a well organised explanation of a wide range of topics, some of which are traditionally hard to master . . . the book is intended to enable students to pass examinations — and this it should well do".   *AUTA*

Manual 1 Contents

Bills of Exchange
Consignments
Joint Ventures
Royalties
Branches
Hire Purchase
Long Term Contracts
Investments
Partnerships
Issue and Redemption of Shares and
    Debentures
Taxation in Accounts

Preparation of Final Accounts of Limited
    Companies for Publication
Statements of Source and Application of
    Funds
Appendices:
    Summary of main disclosure requirements
    of Companies Acts 1948 to 1980
    Statements of Standard Accounting Practice
    (SSAPs) — printed in full
    Answers to section Examination Questions
    Examination Questions with Answers
    Examination Questions without Answers
    Annual Report Example

Manual 2 Contents

Value Added Statements
Financial Statement Analysis and
    Interpretation
Group Profit and Loss Accounts
Group Balance Sheets
Group Statements of Source and
    Application of Funds

Company Amalgamations and Absorptions
Company Reorganisation and Reconstructions
Accounting for Overseas Operations
Accounting for Changing Price Levels
Accounting Standards Committee (Current
    programme)
Stock Exchange Disclosure Requirements

Appendices
Final Accounts of a major and public national company
Companies Act 1981
Answers to Examination Questions
Examination Questions with Answers
Examination Questions without Answers

The author is Senior Lecturer in Accounting, Department of Accounting and Finance, Trent Polytechnic.

Note to Lecturers: Answer Supplement available — see inside front cover of catalogue.

1. 600 pages: 1981: ISBN 0 905435 19 2
2. 500 pages (approx): May 1982: ISBN 0 905435 23 0

Financial Management
R.B. Brockington 2nd Edition

This manual, on the recommended reading list of the ICMA, is intended for students who are preparing to take an examination in Financial Management at final professional level and it will provide them with the knowledge *and the skill in applying it*; both of which they will need to provide a safe pass.

First edition comments:
"Written in note format, the style is very clear and the development logical. There are many worked examples, together with questions and answers from the professional papers. Of great advantage to the professional student is the explanation of approach given clearly in the answers. Few students should be in any doubt as to how the answer was arrived at. In summary, this is a text which is without competitors for the student who is revising for the professional examinations in the subject, and may even prove to be a worthwhile main course text in this context"

Review extract AUTA

"A very strongly recommended text for easy convenient use", "it is liked by students", "explains matters simply and directly"

Lecturers comments

"Makes easy reading and understanding of such an involved subject", "it helped me to pass my examination with an 'A' — it is simple to understand, concise and well presented"

Students comments

Contents

The author is a Lecturer in Finance and Accounting, University of Bath.

Note to Lecturers: Answer Supplement available (see inside front cover of catalogue).

304 pages: 1981: ISBN 0 905435 16 8

Quantitative Techniques
T. Lucey 2nd Edition

This manual is designed to provide a sound understanding of Quantitative Techniques. It is particularly suited to students preparing themselves for the examinations of ICA, ACCA, ICMA and CIPFA (it is prescribed reading for ACCA and ICMA) but is also suitable for students on BEC Higher Level Courses and undergraduates reading Business Studies and allied subjects.

"The book is written in the form of a self-study course with plenty of examples and test exercises. Solutions to the exercises are given at the end of the book. One of the best characteristics of the approach is the use of flowcharts to illustrate the procedural steps for each method, and the whole book has a clarity and a sequential development that are highly desirable in a technical workbook"

review extract British Book News

Contents

The author is Head of the School of Business and Management, Wolverhampton Polytechnic.

Note: 2nd EDITION due for publication in July 1982 has been extensively revised and enlarged to meet the requirements of the Professional Bodies. It includes a major section on appropriate statistical concepts including: Probability, frequency distributions, significance tests, correlation, chi-square and calculus. Many more questions have been included from the Professional Examinations together with fully worked answers. Also, a selection of questions without answers for use by lecturers as assignments (see inside front cover of catalogue).

1st Edition: 352 pages: 1979: ISBN 0 905435 09 5
2nd Edition: 440 pages (approx): July 1982: ISBN 0 905435 27 3

Business Law
K. Abbott   N. Pendlebury

This manual is intended to provide students with a simplified approach to the understanding of Business Law. It covers the examination requirements of the students sitting the following examinations:

ACCA Level 1	—	Law
ICMA Foundation	—	Business Law
ICSA Part 1	—	General Principles of English Law
ICSA Part 2	—	Business Law
ICSA Part 3	—	Industrial Law

It is also relevant to any other students taking an introductory law course e.g. Legal Executives, IAS and BEC.

Contents

Keith Abbott is a Senior Lecturer in Law at Luton College of Higher Education.
Norman Pendlebury has lectured for many years on Law.

Note to Lecturers: Answer Supplement available (see inside front cover of catalogue).

400 pages (approx): May 1982: ISBN 0 905435 22 2

Company Law

K. Abbott

This manual is designed to provide the knowledge required by, primarily, students sitting the ACCA and ICMA examinations in Company Law. Because there are only minor differences between syllabuses, it is also ideally suited to any other student of Company Law, whether at University level or for other professional bodies (e.g. The Law Society, The Institute of Chartered Secretaries and the Institute of Bankers).

Contents

Keith Abbott is a Senior Lecturer in Law at Luton College of Higher Education.

Note to Lecturers: Answer Supplement available (see inside front cover of catalogue).

350 pages (approx): June 1982: ISBN 0 905435 28 1

Economic Analysis

D. Lockwood

The manual provides a comprehensive and in-depth coverage of the work required by students preparing for the following examinations:—

ACCA Section 2 — Managerial Economics
ICMA Professional Stage 1 — Economic Analysis
ICSA Part 4 — Economic Policies and Problems

It may also be useful for those studying economics as part of a non-economics degree course and as secondary reading for 'A' level and Part 1 Economics degree students.

Contents

Introduction to Economic Analysis
Part A. Microeconomics: The Consumer and the Firm:
Allocating Scarce Resources; The Analysis of Demand; The Analysis of Costs; The Conventional Theory of the Firm; The Theory of the Firm; Some Related Issues; The Analysis of Market Power; The Analysis of Oligopoly; The Theory of the Firm Reconsidered; The Growth of Firms; Small Firms; Location of Industry and the Regional Problem; Capital and Investment; Nationalised Industries; Cost Benefit Analysis.

Part B. Macroeconomics: The Economy in General:
The Rise and Fall of Keynesian Economics; The Keynesian Model; The Accelerator; Money, Banking and all that; Stabilising the Economy; Inflation; Policies for Inflation; Unemployment; International Trade I: Why do we Trade with other Countries; International Trade II: The Balance of Payments Accounts; International Trade III: Government Policy; International Trade IV: The Exchange Rate; Planning and Growth; Developing Countries.

Part C. Current Economic Issues:
Are we getting value for the welfare state; The Economic Analysis of Alternatives to the Welfare State; The Taxation Debate; The Eltis/Bacon Thesis; The Economic Analysis of Trade Unions; The Economic Analysis of Marketing; North Sea Oil; The Economic Effects of Micro Technology; Membership of the E.E.C.

Appendices:
Economic Analysis in an examination situation; Outline answers to questions; Questions and Case Studies without Answers.

David Lockwood is Senior Lecturer, Department of Business Studies, West Bromwich College of Commerce and Technology.

Note to Lecturers: Answer Supplement available (see inside front cover of catalogue).

450 pages (approx): June 1982: ISBN 0 905435 29 X

Costing
T. Lucey

This manual is designed to provide a thorough understanding of the theory and practice of cost accountancy. It is particularly relevant to students preparing themselves for the ICA, ACCA, ICMA and CIPFA examinations. Also for students on Foundation Courses in Accounting, Degree and Diploma Courses in Accounting and Business Studies, and for those on BEC courses.

This manual, because of its *instructional* style i.e. building up on previously gained knowledge, makes a unique contribution to costing literature. Too many other books leave students confused as to *when* and *how* they would use costing principles, methods and techniques.

The *clarity* with which the author has written other titles in the series has been favourably commented on. *Its importance cannot be overstated in a subject like costing.*

The author's other titles, Management Information Systems and Quantitative Techniques are prescribed reading for ACCA and ICMA students.

"The book is thoroughly recommended, particularly for students of the professional accountancy bodies . . ."   *The Accountant*

"For its content and clarity this book represents value for money for all students of Costing . . .".   *AUTA*

Contents

The author is Head of the School of Business and Management, Wolverhampton Polytechnic.

Note to Lecturers: Answer Supplement available (see inside front cover of catalogue).

480 pages: 1981: ISBN 0 905435 18 4

Basic Programming

B.J. Holmes

The primary aim of the manual is to teach the BASIC programming language to a depth sufficient to give confidence to any reader requiring a programming knowledge for computer studies examinations to CSE, GCE 'O', 'O/A' and 'A' level, City & Guilds 746 and 747, BEC/TEC National and Higher National Awards, BCS Part I.

It is also ideally suited to those faced with programming for the first time, but who may not be taking any examinations in computer studies e.g. trainee accountants, Business Studies students and 'home computer' enthusiasts.

A vast number of books have been written on BASIC Programming but the need was seen for one which:—

a) Taught good programming habits through "top-down" design and "structured" coding.

b) Included the documentation of programs.

c) Familiarised the reader with the fundamentals of the methodology quickly and used that as a foundation to develop the more complex programming ideas and skills.

d) Was packed with well tried and tested exercises *with answers*, taken from a *wide variety of applications*.

e) Used a Standard for BASIC so that the reader was not confused by trying to deal with every dialect of the language within the text.

Contents

PART ONE — Minimal BASIC
BASIC in Context
Concepts of Flowcharting
Program Flowcharting
Elements of BASIC
Eight Statement BASIC
Elementary Programming
Further Input/Output
Loops, Subroutines and Branching
Arrays
Sorting and Searching Techniques
Mathematics
Project Questions

PART TWO — Further BASIC
String Processing
Validation Techniques
Concepts of File Processing
File Processing
Structured Programming with Comal-80
Design
Case Studies
Project Questions

Appendices

Answers to Questions at end of Chapters
Examination Questions without Answers
ECMA Standard for Minimal BASIC
Specification of COMAL-80
Selection of British Standards Flowchart Symbols
ASC11 · Symbols and codes
EBCDIC Symbols and codes
Comparison of BASIC dialects

The author is a Senior Lecturer in computer studies at Oxford Polytechnic and has taught programming at the various levels required for the examination courses mentioned.

Note to Lecturers: Answer Supplement available (see inside front cover of catalogue).

350 pages (approx): May 1982   ISBN 0905435 25 7

Computer Studies

C.S. French

NEW '82

This manual aims to satisfy the 'O' level, and equivalent Computer Studies text book requirement, and follows the style of Carl French's highly successful 'A' level Computer Science text first published in 1980.

Apart from GCE 'O' level "Computer Studies" the text is eminently suitable for CSE "Computer Studies", BEC General Option "Elements of Data Processing", BEC National Option "Computer Studies", RSA examinations in Computer Studies and TEC units in computer technology.

Included are many examination questions and answers and assignments for course work.

Contents

Introduction
Modern Computers, their General Characteristics
Computer types and their origins
Computer elements and operation

Data, Information. Language and Communication
Data Types and Data Representation
Number Bases
Data Structures and Files
Flowcharts and Program Design
Operations (Arithmetic and Logic)

Hardware Features and Use
From Manual Methods to Modern Systems
Input devices, media, methods and uses
Output devices, media, methods and uses
Storage devices, media, methods and uses
Choice of methods and media

The CPU and its Operation
Elements of the CPU
Program writing and execution
Arithmetic
Logic and Control
Modern system architecture

Software and Programming
Software Types
Program development
Low Level Languages (Features and Programming)
Computational Methods (Programming Techniques)
High Level Languages (Program Structure)
Operating Systems (Purpose and Facilities)

Practical Data Processing
Batch Processing by example
Interactive Systems by example

Applications
Batch, Real-Time, Time Sharing, Bureaux
Application Areas (Science, Dp, Engineering etc)
Organisation and Control Resources

The Social Aspects
Privacy, Jobs etc.
Computers and Society

Appendices
Revision Test Questions, with and without answers
Answers to questions at chapter ends and revision test questions
Course Work and Projects
Details omitted from the text for the sake of clarity
Assignments — suitable for BEC courses

The author is a Senior Lecturer at Hatfield Polytechnic and is also author of "Computer Science".

Note to Lecturers — Answer Supplement available which contains answers to questions at end of Chapters, answers to revision tests and Assignments (see inside front cover of catalogue).

400 pages (approx): June 1982: ISBN 0 905435 24 9

Computer Science

C.S. French

This manual is now in use as text for courses leading to the examination of GCE 'A' level Computer Science, BCS Part 1, City and Guilds and for BEC/TEC.

". . . the coverage is excellent, with plenty of examples and questions . . . a good buy" .

Review extract NATFE.

"Data Processing and Computer Science have a great deal in common, but also possess their exclusive areas of knowledge. A reader wishing to find an introductory work on data processing is well served by the number of excellent texts available, including one from this publisher. Hitherto the same had not been true of computer science, a situation now remedied by this publication . . . the text is eminently readable and is supplemented by useful illustrations, charts, tables and graphs. Each chapter has a helpful selection of self-testing questions to which answers are provided at the end of the book . . . highly recommended". *Review extract AUTA*

"May I congratulate your company and the Author on the publication of 'Computer Science'. At last a down to earth yet authorative summary of GCE and City and Guilds topics". *Lecturer*

"I have recently been informed that I have passed the British Computer Society Part 1 examinations. My success was undoubtedly due to the fact that I used your publication 'Computer Science' during my course of study.

Before I read your book many aspects of computing remained quite vague. However, your treatment of the subject matter and style of writing helped to clear up all the 'hazy' points.

May I congratulate you on what is an excellent piece of work and is without doubt the most useful textbook I have ever used". *Student*

Contents

The author is a Senior Lecturer at Hatfield Polytechnic and has spent a number of years teaching on a wide variety of computer courses. He is also the author of "Computer Studies".

448 pages: 1980: ISBN 0 905435 13 3

Data Processing

E.C. Oliver and R.J. Chapman, (revised by J. Allen) 5th Edition

This manual presents a simplified instructional approach to the understanding of data processing principles. It is extensively used as a Course Textbook on full and part time courses in Polytechnics and Colleges. Prescribed reading for ACCA, ICMA, CIPFA, IAS, SCCA and IDPM students.

"All are to be congratulated on producing an easy to understand manual. They have placed great emphasis on the questions and answers which are split into three types. There are questions with outline answers only, which are intended to test the understanding of points arising out of a particular chapter. There are also examination questions, with comprehensive answers, inserted at the stage where it is considered the student will be best able to give a reasonable answer. Finally, there are progress tests comprising over 60 past examination questions, with answers ranging from mere chapter and section references to comprehensively worked solutions. Many students will find the authors notes on effective study and examination technique helpful . . . . This manual is highly recommended for all those whom it is intended to serve." *Review extract The Accountant.*

"Snappy and no waffle" — *Lecturers comment.*

Contents

Introduction to Data Processing
Organisation and Methods
Conventional Methods
Small Computers
Introduction to EDP and Computers
Hardware
Computer Files
Data Collection and Controls
Programming and Software
Flowcharts and Decision Tables
Systems Analysis
Applications
Management of EDP

Appendices
    Outline Answers to Questions set at the
      end of Chapters
    Comprehensive Answers to Examination
      Questions
    Progress Tests (Questions and Answers)
    Examination Questions without Answers
    Detail Omitted from the text in the
      interests of clarity
    Using the Questions and Answers in
      the manual
    Effective Study/Examination Technique

E.C. Oliver and R.J. Chapman are partners in DP Publications. J. Allen is Principal Lecturer in Management Information Systems and Data Processing at South West London College.

Note to Lecturers: Answer Supplement available (see inside front cover of catalogue).

336 pages: 1981: ISBN 0 905435 15 X